TRACING VILLAINS AND THEIR VICTIMS

FAMILY HISTORY FROM PEN & SWORD

TRACING VILLAINS AND THEIR VICTIMS

A Guide to Criminal Ancestors for Family Historians

Jonathan Oates

Pen & Sword
FAMILY HISTORY

First published in Great Britain in 2017
PEN & SWORD FAMILY HISTORY
an imprint of
Pen & Sword Books Ltd
47 Church Street,
Barnsley South Yorkshire, S70 2AS

ISBN 978 1 47389 256 9

A CIP catalogue record for this book is
available from the British Library.

Typeset in Palatino and Optima by CHIC GRAPHICS

Printed and bound in England by
CPI Group (UK), Croydon, CR0 4YY

Pen & Sword Books Ltd incorporates the imprints of Pen & Sword
Archaeology, Atlas, Aviation, Battleground, Discovery, Family History,
History, Maritime, Military, Naval, Politics, Railways, Select, Social History,
Transport, True Crime, Claymore Press, Frontline Books, Leo Cooper,
Praetorian Press, Remember When, Seaforth Publishing and Wharncliffe.

For a complete list of Pen & Sword titles please contact
PEN & SWORD BOOKS LTD
47 Church Street, Barnsley, South Yorkshire, S70 2AS, England
E-mail: enquiries@pen-and-sword.co.uk
Website: www.pen-and-sword.co.uk

CONTENTS

ACKNOWLEDGEMENTS

Paul Lang, has, as ever, allowed me to use some of his postcards from his vast collection for this book and so I wholeheartedly thank him once again. I would also like to thank both Paul and John Gauss for their time and trouble in reading through a draft of this book and their many useful comments. This book is dedicated to Paul and his family.

INTRODUCTION

The popular pastime of family history can throw up interesting and perhaps famous names; the hunt for noble or even royal ancestors is sometimes cited as a reason for a genealogical hunt. Yet apart from the search for the illustrious in our family's past, there is the possibility – in fact a rather stronger one – of finding what were once known as 'black sheep'. These may not be ancestors one wants to admit to having, but if they are sufficiently in the past, we may well sympathise with them. An ancestor who was shipped to Australia for sheep stealing? Doubtless a poor man merely wanting to feed his family – or perhaps part of an organised gang who stole for profit?

My own story about a criminal ancestor is perhaps a little tenuous, but my grandmother's sister married one of the men who was to become one of the Great Train Robbers of 1963. I usually quickly add that this was George Wheater, the solicitor who arranged the acquisition of the farmhouse in Buckinghamshire for the gang and not someone who did anything violent. After receiving a relatively short sentence in gaol for his involvement in the heist he was asked how he found prison? 'Not too bad', he said, 'but I did not like having to mix with criminals!' At least that is how the family legend goes.

Many people will have criminals in their ancestry and this book will help you to find out about them. Indeed, there is more information about those accused of crime than there is about people who apparently led perfectly blameless lives in the legal sense of the word. This is because the agents of the state and church take notice of those who break the state's rules. Records are created about those entangled in the justice system at the level of trials, prisons, the police and other sources. Crime has been a major concern throughout the ages and seems to be an inescapable part of the human condition ever since Cain.

The building blocks for family history research – parish registers, records of civil registration from 1837, census returns, possibly military records and wills – will provide evidence for ancestors' lives, but these are mere frameworks. The criminal or victim who is an ancestor will generate far more. These will naturally provide information about their involvement with crime, but most will provide additional facts. Both newspapers and those investigating the crime or dealing with trials not only look at narrowly defined behaviour, but often concern themselves with other matters about an individual: physical descriptions, educational background and religious, even political behaviour, relationships with family, friends, colleagues and enemies, hobbies and interests, mental health and

The Deed. Paul Lang's Collection

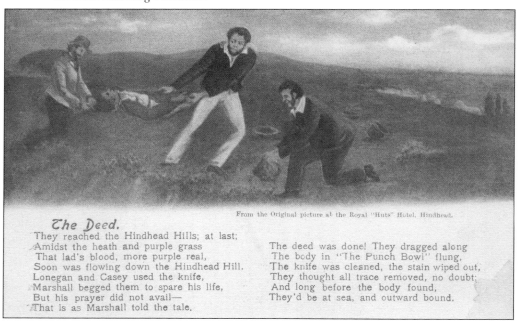

From the Original picture at the Royal "Huts" Hotel, Hindhead.

The Deed.

They reached the Hindhead Hills; at last;
Amidst the heath and purple grass
That lad's blood, more purple real,
Soon was flowing down the Hindhead Hill.
Lonegan and Casey used the knife,
Marshall begged them to spare his life,
But his prayer did not avail—
That is as Marshall told the tale.

The deed was done! They dragged along
The body in "The Punch Bowl" flung,
The knife was cleaned, the stain wiped out,
They thought all trace removed, no doubt;
And long before the body found,
They'd be at sea, and outward bound.

other habits, likes and dislikes. There may even be photographs, perhaps in prison garb or as a mugshot or even as a corpse.

However, what constitutes crime has altered considerably over the centuries, as have punishments for those found guilty. Some aspects of human behaviour have always been deemed criminal – murder, manslaughter, rape, theft, burglary, riot, sedition, fraud and forgery for instance. Others once fell within the bounds of criminal behaviour but no longer do so: suicide, abortion, witchcraft, homosexual acts between men. Religious and moral offences are no longer deemed actionable. Then there are others which are now criminal but which were not always so, such as taking certain drugs, such as laudanum or Sherlock Holmes's stimulant of choice, cocaine, or speaking or writing certain words in public liable to offend.

Wartime often leads to new regulations, such as the Defence of the Realm Act of 1915 which created more offences. During the world wars, one could offend by not having house lights blacked out, or for activities related to rationing. It was against the law for servicemen to keep diaries or for cameras to be used. Spreading rumours could also be deemed illegal. There were clampdowns on drinking in pubs. In earlier centuries 'seditious language' (speaking out against the monarch or his/her government) could incur the wrath of a magistrate if it were overheard.

This book aims to guide the reader through the sources available in researching criminal ancestors. As a general rule, the more heinous the crime, the more information will be available. The theft of apples from an orchard might merit a sentence or two; the activities of a serial killer will result in pages and pages of information. In between these two extremes the amount of text dedicated to a criminal will vary considerably.

The book is organised not by type of offence/offender, as in *Tracing Your Criminal Ancestors* by Stephen Wade, nor does it go into detail about these offences, but rather it examines the type of record which will provide useful information to researchers into ancestors whose lives have been affected by crime whether as perpetrator or

The Arrest

From the Original Picture at the "Royal Huts" Hotel. Hindhead.

But vengeance soon was on their track,
And quickly brought the murderers back;
A shepherd chanced that way to stray
And saw the murdered sailor lay.
He went for help and gave alarms,
When all the country people arms

And follows in the villains' wake,
They reach "The Flying Bull," at Rake,
The law's strong guardian soon was there,
And brought them back to Hazelmere.
When justice sat and law was read—
"Condemn them to be hung till dead"

The Arrest. Paul Lang's Collection

as victim. It does not deal with the agents of law and order, such as police officers and legal officials, either. Chapter 1 looks at the criminal courts of England: manorial, quarter sessions, assizes, crown and magistrates' courts. Assize courts dealt with a variety of serious crimes in past centuries. I have avoided having chapters on numerous types of crime which constantly refer to the same series of records. Chapter 2 deals with other courts in Great Britain; church courts and courts martial, but also those courts unique to different parts of the kingdom: Wales, Scotland and the island jurisdictions. Chapter 3 deals with the records of various punishments – transportation, executions and prisons. Chapter 4 is an examination of police records. Chapter 5 deals with the myriad information to be found in newspapers. There is then a chapter examining contemporary and modern books which include useful information about crimes. The final chapter contains miscellaneous sources not easily fitted elsewhere.

Whilst it is common to focus entirely on the criminal, it is important not to forget the victims of crime who are often overlooked or marginalised. The author recently read an autobiographical magazine article by a reformed killer in which there was much about the man himself, but though it was mentioned that he had killed twice, not even the names of those two people were given (which in itself gives an insight into the criminal mind). Information provided about crime does focus on the criminal, but there is usually information about the victim/s, and they too are someone's ancestors. They must not be forgotten.

Victims tend to feature less in records. This is because the emphasis of the state is to deal with the offender and so he or she is the one tried in court before undergoing punishment. Victims may appear at the beginning of a case, perhaps because they have been robbed, defrauded, raped or murdered and if alive will probably be called as a witness at the trial, but they can often remain a peripheral figure. Yet even so, by their involvement in a crime, they will warrant more attention than someone who is utterly uninvolved.

At the end of the book are worked examples of a criminal and a victim, showing examples of the myriad sources which can be used to flesh out their lives. There is also a list of useful addresses and

The National Archives, Kew. The Author

books. One abbreviation which is often employed in this book is TNA (the National Archives), which is a place that most family historians will need to have dealings with.

The author has had eight books about real-life crime and three biographies of post-war killers published, so is knowledgeable about the sources for criminal history, especially as regards London and its environs.

Edwardian era police officer. Author's collection

Chapter 1

CRIMINAL COURTS OF ENGLAND

Those accused of crime, if arrested and charged (the second does not necessarily follow), will probably face trial as a defendant. At the trial the court will determine whether the defendant is guilty or not and if the former, will receive sentence; if the latter, they will go free. There are and were numerous types of court, depending on the time period in question and the nature of the offence. This chapter will deal with civil criminal courts in England. Clearly the focus of the courts is the defendant, whom the case is brought against, but the victim will also be involved as evidence will be given by them, unless they are deceased and then evidence will probably be given about them and their life, especially the latter stages of it. If the defendant is found guilty then punishment will be meted out and for that see Chapter 3.

Court proceedings usually begin very shortly after the apprehension of those thought culpable of the crime, often a day or two after the arrest has been made and the defendant or defendants charged. Sentence can be passed within days of the arrest if it is a relatively minor one where only one hearing is necessary with a minimum of witnesses needed and often no jury. However, in serious cases, where a great deal of evidence has to be gone through, the length of the judicial process can be extremely time-consuming; months may pass by in some cases, or even years in more recent decades.

Note that none of the sources examined below, which chiefly serve to give an administrative framework of the trial, will present you with a transcript of what was actually said in court. The majority of cases did not have this recorded. A handful of very important cases from the sixteenth to the twentieth century were transcribed and published as *Notable British Trials*. There is also the Howells' *Complete State Trials* which deals with treason trials from 1163–1820, and, to a lesser extent, *Celebrated Trials*. These mostly deal with murder and treason and are discussed in Chapter 6, as are the Proceedings of the Old Bailey. The other source is the newspapers where truncated versions of what was said are published and for these see Chapter 5. We shall examine the courts in roughly chronological order.

MANORIAL COURTS

From at least the eleventh century everyone in England lived in a territorial unit known as a manor. Most of the inhabitants would hold their land as tenants to their landlord who would in turn hold it from a more senior holder, often a baron or a bishop. To administer these manors, there were two types of regularly held court which freeholders were obliged to attend.

These were the courts baron and the courts leet. Both were made up of manorial tenants who dealt with issues arising from the actions of their fellow tenants. The former was chiefly concerned with the transfer of land, but the latter, which met every six months or so, dealt with petty theft, affray, drunkenness, trespass and so forth. Most are written in Latin and can date from the thirteenth to the seventeenth centuries. Not all survive. They can be found by using the Manorial Deeds Register online at the TNA website by typing in the name of the manor or parish whose records are sought. Most are held at the appropriate county record office, but not necessarily; colleges at Oxford and Cambridge held many manors and so the manorial records will be in the appropriate college library. A few can be seen online, such as those for Wakefield from 1274 to 1297 at http://tinyurl.com/yh4cag9.

The following are some examples taken from the late medieval court rolls of the manor of Northolt in Middlesex.

They also say that Ralph Ellys, William Harte, William

Manorial Court, Long Crendon. Author.

Shepherde, Matthew Vincent, Thomas Hedger and George Vyncente have broken the regulations by putting their animals in the common fields in the Stuble of the manor and they are to be fined 2d for each animal.

George Pym fined 5s for trespassing on the lord's demesne by cutting down and spoiling a whelme at Thistelehame Gate.

Marion Admond is a common tippler and sells ale in unsealed measures. Fines 2d.

Also they present that John Admond has assaulted John Vyncent against the peace of the lord king. He is in mercy as shown.

Details are sparse, but these are the only surviving records for many ancestors prior to the introduction of parish registers in the sixteenth century. Manorial courts fell into decline in the sixteenth century but in some cases were still held until the abolition of the manor as a legal entity in the early twentieth century. Other courts, however, became more important, and we will turn to these.

STAR CHAMBER

Another ancient court, originating from the Middle Ages, revived in 1487 and which continued in harness until its abolition in 1641, was the Court of Star Chamber. It was named after the painted stars on the ceiling of the chamber in the royal palace of Westminster where the Privy Council met in the fourteenth and fifteenth centuries. The court dealt with many local disputes between individuals and depositions were often lengthy. Disputes were over matters such as issues of public disorder, forcible entry into properties, assaults and quarrels over property rights. The court also dealt with officials accused of corruption. Records are held at TNA in STAC1-9, arranged by reign. They provide increasing levels of information from 1558, which reflect their increasing activity; 150 hearings per year in the sixteenth century and over 700 per year in the seventeenth.

They can be searched on TNA's online catalogue under plaintiff (the person bringing the case to court) and defendant to give an archival reference of the relevant document. The documents can then be ordered at TNA as they are not available online. Unlike many legal documents prior to 1733 they are written in English. The papers which exist are the case papers or proceedings, including pleadings by both parties, with answers and rejoinders, lists of questions put to witnesses and their depositions and examinations. The great problem is that the order and decree books which outline the judgments on the cases in question are missing. Documents in E159 record fines imposed from 1596 to 1641 and so these will indicate the results in some cases (i.e. the losing party will pay the fine).

A case from a sixteenth-century Star Chamber Court case in Cheshire ran as follows:

To the King, our soveren lorde, and to his most honourable

and discrete councell. Petously complayneth Elizabeth Whykstede, wedowe of Thomas Whykstede, that whereas on the 3rd of January last past the said Elizabeth was at her dwelling house of Whykstede within your county pales of Cheshire, one John Maynwaring the elder and Thomas Morall, with six other armed persons riotously broke into her said house, and there fynding your said subject and her chylderne to the nombre of ten chylderne with his in their beddes, did forcibly take one of her saud chylderne callyd Hugh Whykstede (being but of nine yeres old) nakyd out of his bed, and carryd him out of your said Cheshire pales into your countie of Shropshire, where they yet kepe hym in some place unknowen …

The defendants answer that the said Thomas Whykstede held by knight service and a rent of 1d from George, Erle of Shrewisburye, two menses and forty acres of land in Whykstede, Wriswall and Bradley. As servants of the said Erle, without any branch of the peace, they went to Wykestede to fetch the said Hugh, being under age and heir to his father, and brought him to the same Erle to the castle of Sheffield.

A number of county record societies have published some of the Star Chamber proceedings from their counties. These are those for Cheshire from the reign of Henry VIII and for Somerset from 1485–1547. Yorkshire Star Chamber Proceedings have been published by the Yorkshire Archaeological Society and a selection of cases appears in G R Elton's book *Star Chamber Stories*. These can be found in County Record Offices (CROs) and at TNA's library.

The court system in England from the later Middle Ages to the 1970s was a two-tier system. The lower court was the quarter and petty sessions for counties and incorporated towns and the upper court was the assizes (or Central Criminal Court/Old Bailey for Middlesex/London). The majority of offenders would go before the lower courts.

QUARTER SESSIONS COURTS

A longer lasting institution than the Star Chamber was the Quarter Sessions, which was established in each English county and in county boroughs. This was formed of men (and women in the twentieth century) appointed as Justices of the Peace (JP), an office instituted in 1361. They were usually drawn from the ranks of the gentry, and in later years, the clergy, or in urban districts professionals and merchants. In the sixteenth century the office became of greater importance as governments passed on the burden on administering their legislation in the counties as they met four times a year to deal with both administrative (until the establishment of the county councils in 1888) and criminal matters. The JPs were amateur and not necessarily legally trained but were usually educated men, chosen for their social standing and often political reliability. They tried cases without the benefit of a jury at their quarterly sessions (four times a year), but in the nineteenth century some counties had intermediate sessions which met in between these four times. They often met at the county town, so Wakefield in the case of the West Riding of Yorkshire. Furthermore, they could also mete out summary justice if one or two of them were present (known as petty sessions).

Some counties have more than one sessions court; Middlesex had one (1549–1971), which covered London up to 1889 and thereafter the reduced county of Middlesex, but there was also the Westminster Sessions from 1681 to 1844 which also included part of central London. From 1889 to 1971 there was the London Sessions Court covering offences in the newly formed county of London (inner London). The City of London had its own court as well, and that has always been outside the jurisdiction of the other London courts just mentioned.

Some towns and cities had their separate court of quarter sessions; some dating from the Middle Ages, such as York, for instance, as defined by the city's charter. So, although an urban district is physically within a county, those committing offences within its boundaries will be dealt with at the town/city quarter sessions, which operated in the same way as the county sessions did, though the magistrates were usually merchants and professionals rather than gentlemen. Records will be held at the city archives or county record office where appropriate. For instance, those for York are at York City Archives, whereas those for Beverley are at East Riding Record Office in Beverley. Records of the quarter sessions for the boroughs of Abingdon, Maidenhead, Wallingford and Windsor are at Berkshire Record Office.

There was no hard and fast rule as to which types of offence were dealt with by quarter sessions and which by the assizes (the higher courts; see later in this chapter), but these courts could not sentence the guilty to death. A lot would depend on convenience and cost and when the crime took place. Quarter sessions would tend to deal with lesser offences, but these could be rated differently in different times. After 1832, for instance, sheep stealing ceased to be a capital offence and so sheepstealers were dealt with by the JPs. Sentences they imposed would be the lesser ones: fines, limited transportation, flogging and branding and, increasingly from the nineteenth century, imprisonment.

Few quarter session records survive for the fourteenth and fifteenth centuries; those that do are held at TNA, in JUST1. Putman's *Proceedings before the Justices of the Peace in the Fourteenth and Fifteenth Centuries* list them. The bulk of quarter session records, however, date from the sixteenth century and are held at county or borough record offices. For listings see J S W Gibson's *Quarter Session Records for Family Historians*. Or check the website of the appropriate CRO.

The major series of records are the Order Books (usually termed Minute Books from the late eighteenth century) and the indictment books/rolls, which list those who were brought before them, with a note of the verdict. There may also be prison records as prisons were a responsibility of 'local government' until 1877 when the Home Office took over the task as it was felt that central government would be more effective. Those composed prior to 1733 may be in Latin, but most of the documents need not be translated as the key pieces of information are name and parish, offence, verdict and date.

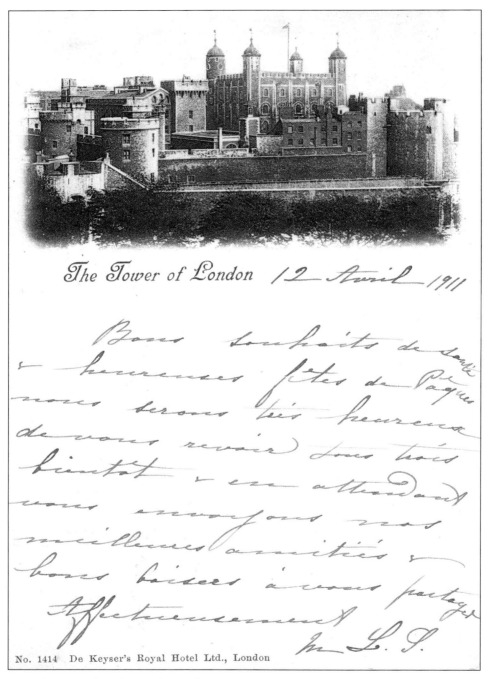

The Tower of London. *Author's collection*

An example from the Middlesex Sessions Rolls is as follows:

Reginald Bucknall is convicted for forging and publishing a letter of attorney; and the will of Jacob Jacobson. He is fined 3/4, and is to stand in and upon the pillory three several days for one hour, between 9 AM and 12 o'clock noon: the first day upon Little Tower Hill, the second near the Sun Tavern, in Ratcliffe Highway, and the third day near Ratcliffe Cross, with a paper over his head showing his offence. He is committed to New prison (without bail of mainprize) until the next Sessions, and until he pay the fine and undergo the punishment, then to be delivered, paying his fees, 10/4

Some examples of indictments from the Easter Sessions of 1705 for the Buckinghamshire Quarter Sessions are as follows:

• Robert James of Great Marlowe, bargeman, for assaulting Elizabeth, wife of John Langley.
• Thomas Pargiter of Sherrington, grazier, for a nuisance in the highways between Olney and Wooburne.
• Jane, wife of Richard Johnson, of Beirton, carpenter, for stealing three hens from Finch Howes, gentleman.
• William Phillips of Great Marlowe, husbandman, for assaulting Mary, wife of Thomas Harris.

The same court also recorded 'Informations', effectively depositions, about criminal behaviour and an example from the summer session for the same year is as follows:

By Mary, wife of Henry Stone, collar maker, Humphrey Newton, innholder and Dorothy Humphrey, widow, all of Aylesbury, and Thomas Stevens, butcher, and Richard Charge, sawyer, both of Wendover, who stated that at Aylesbury on the 9th may and 'being the Day of Electing Burgesses', they saw Mr Hampden and Mr Shute riding down the street in horseback, followed by Sir Roger Hall in a coach. There was a large crowd in the street and they saw Thomas Hawkins, John Horwood, John Rance and John Mildmay throw stones and brickbats at the gentlemen, and threatened them with sticks and incite the Crowd by shouting 'Knock them on the Head, Beat the Rogues' Brains out'. Mary Stone and Dorothy Humphrey were in Henry Stone's house with Amy Bayley and Thomas Stevens was in John Green's house.

Recognisances, which are agreements for a form of bail, often exist in large numbers. These are bonds signed by a JP to secure a named person's appearance at the next sessions court. Usually the sureties for the person's appearance and bail payments are also noted.

The following is an example from the East Riding Quarter Sessions:

> discharged
> East Riding of the County of York – to wit
> Be it remembered that this third day of July one thousand seven hundred and forty six, Henry Welburn of Coniston in the riding aforesd, servant, personally came before me one of his Majestyes justices of the peace for the said Riding, also James Hardy and Robert Carrick of Coniston aforesaid and acknowledged themselves indebted unto our Sovereigne Lord the King (to witt) the said Henry Welburn in one hundred Pounds, the said James Hardy, and the said Robert Carrick in fifty pounds each of good and lawfull money of Great Britain to be levied upon their Goods and Chattles, Lands and Tenements to the use and behoofe of our said Sovereigne Lord the King if default shall be made in the following Condition.
> The Condition of the above Recognizance is such that if the above named Henry Welburn shall Personally appear at the next General Quarter Sessions of the peace to be held at Beverley, for the east Riding of the County of York, to be accountable for speaking Certain Seditious Words at Preston

in the said Riding, and that the said Henry Welburn in the meantime be of Good behaviour and not depart the court without leave then this Recognizance shall be void or else to remain in full force and virtue.

Taken and acknowledged before me the day and year first above written.

Hugh Bethell

Many quarter session records, especially for the fourteenth and sixteenth centuries, have been calendared and published by the appropriate county records society. These are usually indexed by name so can be searched quickly and easily. They can be found on the open shelves of the county record office library or in the library of TNA. However, they rarely cover the later eighteenth century to the twentieth century.

Those published as are follows: Buckinghamshire (1678–1712, 3 volumes), Dorset Order Books (1625–38), Durham (1471–1625), Cheshire (1559–1760), Middlesex (1558–1709), Northampton (1314–16, 1320, 1630, 1657–8), Oxfordshire Order Books (1614–37), Somerset (1603–85, 4 volumes), Surrey (1659–66), Sussex (1642–9), Warwickshire Order Books (1625–95, 9 volumes), Warwickshire and Coventry (1377–97), Wiltshire Order Books (1642–54), North Riding of Yorkshire (1605–1750), West Riding of Yorkshire (1597–1602, 1611–42), York Civic Records (1474–1588, 8 volumes) and Yorkshire Sessions (1361–4).

A few are available online. For example, the Lancashire Quarter Session records and petitions from 1648 to 1908 can be viewed on Ancestry and can be searched by name.

Quarter sessions records include calendars of prisoners awaiting trial, which are listings for each sessions. These include names, charges and the JP who made the committal. Some may include name/s of witness/es and date of discharge or sentence. These may be called gaol delivery books or registers. Some have separate listings of debtors; Bedfordshire Quarter Sessions records include rolls of debtors from 1770 to 1854.

There may also be registers of appeals. These are not just for those unhappy with their sentence but also licensing appeals and poor law settlement cases, reflecting the fact that up to 1889 quarter sessions was as much an administrative unit of local government as a criminal court.

By the nineteenth century these records can be quite detailed. They often include examinations of defendants and of witnesses, known as depositions. These can detail the crime/s in question and the behaviour of the accused. Order books then give the court's verdict on the defendant and the sentence pronounced. Records are usually arranged chronologically.

Quarter sessions records can exist in great number and are usually organised by the record creator. The treasurer's records often include payments relating to crime. For example, following an Act of 1824, payments could be made to prisoners discharged from gaol in order for them to return to their parish of settlement. The LMA has accounts, passes and receipts for such former prisoners for the period 1832–66. There are also receipts for witness' expenses from 1805–83. There is also a Book of Informations, which are notes made from reports of informers, chiefly about people transgressing the trading and licensing laws, noting offender, occupation, date, charge and later notes of any court appearance. Petitions and depositions can also exist.

PETTY SESSIONS
It had always been possible for one or two JPs to dole out more or less summary justice to miscreants between sittings of quarter sessions, but by the end of the eighteenth century this arrangement became known as petty sessions and began to be better recorded.

Also known as Magistrates' Courts, and by novelists and journalists as police courts (presumably to differentiate them from civil courts and to note that they deal with crime, even though they are not run by the police), these were the lowest rung of the judicial ladder. Due to the rise in population and the relative infrequency of quarter sessions hearings, many towns were served by newly

Ealing Magistrates' Court. The Author

established magistrates' courts (in London and its environs, following the Metropolitan Magistrates' Act of 1839), which would convene on weekdays to deal with the heavy volume of 'petty' offences. The defendant usually came before the JP a day or two after being arrested and was one of several people whose case was heard each day. These hearings took place without a jury, though the defendant may have been represented by a solicitor. The punishments they were able to impose were gaol sentences (though not with hard labour or corporal punishment) and fines.

Magistrates' courts may also, after a number of hearings, commit those accused of a serious offence to a higher court (usually the assizes). Thomas Gray and Jack Field were before the magistrates' courts at Hailsham in September and October 1920 as the case for murder was being made against them, before being committed to trial at the assizes for December.

The records they produced are principally court registers and each court could have more than one sitting. The registers show a minimum of information: date of case, name and occupation of defendant, offence, witness/es and sentence if any. For instance, the Marlborough Street Magistrates' Court in London, on 26 May 1949 had one Ronald Chesney before them. Describing himself as 'a writer', he was charged with being 'knowingly concerned in dealing with goods to wit, 222 pairs of nylon stockings with intent to defraud' at Bourton Street, W1. He was found guilty and given the option of a fine of £25 and three months in prison or nine months in prison. Lacking money, he spent time in prison, being released on 25 January 1950, after having been given a remission of a few weeks.

They are rarely indexed by name of defendant, so unless a rough date of the hearing is known, searching can be a lengthy process. They are, however, comprehensive and each case will be recorded here. Records are held at the appropriate county record office that covers that court's jurisdiction. For instance, Hailsham's and Eastbourne's court records are held at East Sussex Record Office near Brighton and those for most London courts are at the LMA. Often lengthy closure periods have been imposed on these classes of records; at East Sussex there is a closure period of a century on the basis that some of those charged nearly a century ago might well be alive and aged over 110.

In the case of all courts, the records will rarely state where the imprisonment is to take place; often in the county gaol but not necessarily so.

ASSIZE COURTS

At the top end of the judicial system of courts from the fourteenth century to 1971, England, outside London and Middlesex, was divided into six assize circuits (Home, Midland, Western, Oxford, Northern and Norfolk), usually comprised of a small number of adjacent counties. From 1830 Wales was incorporated into this system; being divided into four circuits (Chester, North Wales, Carmarthen and Brecon). London and Middlesex were under the Central Criminal Court, known as the Old Bailey, which met ten times a year to reflect the heavier workload (in the seventeenth and eighteenth century assize courts met twice a year, rising to thrice in the nineteenth century). There was some modification of the boundaries of these districts in the late nineteenth century. A number of professional judges would tour each circuit twice a year to hear the cases brought before them, and a jury would be empanelled to hear the case and decide on a verdict which had to be unanimous. The assizes would hear cases which took place within their particular jurisdiction, so a murder in East Sussex would be heard at the court house of the county town (Lewes). They were authorised to act from the commissions of gaol delivery, of the peace and of oyer and terminer (meaning to listen and to determine). They tried those held in the county gaol or who were on bail. Cases before them included treason, riot, rebellion, coining, murder, burglary and other offences.

A trial is an adversarial legal contest presided over by a judge, who will be an experienced barrister. The defendant will be represented by a barrister in court, who will have been briefed by the defendant's solicitor (who will have represented him in the lower court). The case is deemed to be on behalf of the Crown and will also be represented by a barrister. Those unable to afford one will be provided one out of legal aid (usually fairly junior) but the wealthy or those whom a newspaper has decided to support, usually use a renowned criminal barrister, such as Sir Edward Marshall Hall in the early twentieth century or David Maxwell Ffye in the mid-century. Both barristers may be supported by a junior colleague. The defendant's barrister will advise on the plea by the defendant (not just guilty and not guilty, but also guilty but insane, guilty of manslaughter and so on) and will interview them on numerous occasions. Both sides will consult all the police evidence and interview witnesses prior to the trial.

At the trial itself, the clerk of the court reads out the indictment and the defendant makes their plea. There is an opening speech by the prosecution, then the prosecuting barrister interviews his witnesses, which could include police officers, pathologists and lay witnesses. The defence can then cross-examine each one before they leave the witness box. The defence next makes its opening speech, and examines its witnesses. This could include after 1905 the defendant (who, prior to that date, could not speak on their own behalf for it was considered that they would automatically lie). They are then cross-examined by the prosecution – often a difficult time for the defendant. When all witnesses are done with, the prosecution makes its final address to the jury of twelve people (including women after 1918) who have heard all the court proceedings; followed by the defence. Then the judge makes his charge to the jury, pointing out the parts of the case they have to particularly bear in mind. He may lean towards one side or another if the evidence suggests that is reasonable. The jury then leave the court to discuss what they have heard (these discussions are never made public nor recorded) and return once a decision has been reached. Until the 1960s this had to be unanimous but thereafter a majority verdict is permissible. Once the jury foreman tells the judge the verdict, the judge passes sentence on that result. The defendant may comment but rarely does.

The assize courts passed heavier sentences, such as lengthy sentences of transportation (up to 1867) and execution (up to 1964). They could, until the 1940s, pass prison sentences which included hard labour, especially when the offender had already been convicted previously or was convicted of an offence whilst on probation.

The archives of the assize courts are held at TNA. Although the assize system began in the later twelfth century, there are few archives for the earlier years of their existence. Records which do survive for the fourteenth and fifteenth centuries are to be found in series JUST3, 1, 4 and KB9. The bulk of assize papers are in the sequence ASSI. There are a number of different types of record which may survive: indictments, witness statements, gaol calendars, recognisances and minute books.

Indictments set out the offence with which the defendant is accused. Until 1733 the document will be in abbreviated Latin. They appear to be quite useful, giving name, occupation and parish of origin, as well as the offence. However, the occupation of the defendant, until the late eighteenth century will be 'labourer' and the parish will be the parish that the crime was committed in. Furthermore, the legal phraseology often makes it quite difficult to ascertain the alleged offence. Later assize indictments are more accurate.

Witness statements taken before the trial are known as depositions. They will be in English, but from the early nineteenth to the mid-twentieth century most of the witness statements no longer exist, except for those cases dealing with the most serious offences such as murder or treason. More recent deposition files may contain additional material such as photographs, maps and appeal papers.

Minute books are also known as Crown or gaol books and provide useful summaries of the trials held before the court in question. They are in date order, listing defendant and charge, and usually state the verdict and sentence. They are not indexed and the handwriting can be quite difficult to read until one is used to it. Unless a researcher has a rough idea of the date of the trial, it can be a time-consuming endeavour.

Old Assizes Court, Winchester. The Author

A nineteenth-century example from the Bedfordshire Assizes for 1855 reads as follows:

10 March	Thomas Perry Conf. hl. 2cm	5th Jany. Steals 20lbs wt of coals of Richard Stokes.
	William Foote Conf. sent. hl. 6cm	17th July at Eaton Socon being in DH of Ursula Grubbard and steals 2 flannel shirts of 4 handfs and 2 pairs of stockings of Francis Joyce and 6 pieces of calico 1 night gown and a smelling bottle of Sarah Joyce.
	George Knight Conf. hl. 6cm	15th Jany. At Laton uttering a counterfeit shilling to Thomas Wilsher and a fraud on same day and place uttering another counterfeit shilling to Emma Gurny.

Another example, as noted in the Old Bailey Court for 1941 was that of Donald Hume (1919–98). He had been arrested at RAF Northolt on 3 April 1941 when he tried to cash a cheque for £25. It was refused and he was arrested by officers of the Special Branch. On his arrest it was noted that he was five feet and a half inches in height, with grey eyes, dark brown hair and a chest measuring 32 inches. Hume was convicted on 13 May 1941, but confessed and was bailed on recognisances for £5. He appeared at the Old Bailey on 24 June. He was charged with falsely suggesting he was in the RAF, wearing a RAF uniform to gain false entry and forging false entry documents. The witnesses against him were Frank Charles Faiers, Edward Lennox Scott-Atkinson, Patrick Pullen and Detective George Helps. The counsel at the court was rising barrister Christmas Humphreys (who ironically was the prosecuting KC at his trial for murder nine years later). Here Hume was deemed 'an undesirable and unreliable

The Old Bailey. Author's collection

character', but was given a lenient sentence, probably in part because of his youth and because it was his first known offence, in being bound over for two years. He was also fined the token sum of £5 and was ordered to undergo psycho-therapeutical treatment but never went.

Then there are the indictments. These can be difficult to handle up to the end of the nineteenth century, for they are very large parchment documents and very unwieldy. There is usually a very helpful printed Calendar of Prisoners, listing defendants and the crime they are accused of, with much detail on both. The 1848 spring Assizes for Cambridge gives the following for the first entry:

1. Henry Cooper, aged 23, Liverpool, tin-plate worker and George Andrews, aged 26, Birmingham. Labourer. Property on arrest: None.

Committed Aug. 2nd, 1847 by the Rev. William Law, charged on the oath of Thomas Gadd of Wimpole, labourer, and others, with having, about the hour of ten on the night of

19

the 31st of July last, burglariously broken and entered the dwelling house of the said Thomas Gadd and feloniously stole one coat, one waistcoat and one pair of shoes the property of Thomas Gadd.

The indictment itself is a printed form with the details of each case written in by hand, often repeating some of those from the calendar. The one for the aforesaid Cooper gives the costs of the items he stole – ten shillings for the coat, sixpence for the waistcoat and eighteen pence for the shoes. It notes that he was found guilty and sentenced to ten years' transportation.

The survival of these records as outlined above is very variable. There are indictments from 1559 for Surrey and Sussex, but these documents do not commence until the seventeenth or eighteenth century for some counties and, in a few cases, not until the early nineteenth century. Few depositions predate the eighteenth century and for some counties many do not exist prior to the following century.

It should be noted that there were no indexes to these documents. Unless a date is known searching them can be a lengthy task. Information is often duplicated within these records if several exist for the case that you are interested in. There are also closure periods on these documents of seventy-five years as a rule.

There are other papers associated with assizes. These are the sheriffs' vouchers from 1758 to 1832, held at TNA in E370/35-51. The sheriff was the county official responsible for the upkeep of the county gaol. The vouchers record information about prisoners awaiting trial at the assizes, noting how long they had been in prison, their sentence and the cost of maintaining them in prison.

Some assize records for the Middle Ages have been published in county record series. Those which exist are as follows: Lancashire (1202–85, 2 volumes), Lincolnshire (1202–9) and Northampton (1202–3). Trials in the sixteenth century for the Home Circuit (Essex, Hertfordshire, Kent, Surrey and Sussex) have been indexed in the Calendar of Assize Records.

Indictments from Essex Assizes from 1558 to 1714 can be found online at the Essex Record Office's website. The texts of the trials at the Old Bailey, which is the assize court for London and Middlesex from 1678 to 1913 are available online at www.oldbaileyonline.org They can be searched by name (of defendant, victim or witness), offence and place. A fuller discussion of this source appears in Chapter 6.

PALATINE JURISDICTIONS
The term palatine means 'pertaining to a place'. In the eleventh and twelfth centuries the Norman kings established several border districts of their kingdom of England to be held by a powerful individual, such as the Prince Bishop of Durham or the Earl of Chester. These counties were thus outside the assize system. These were the palatine jurisdictions of Cheshire, Durham and Lancashire, or in the city of Bristol. These operated in the same way that the assize courts did and their archives are held at TNA.

JUVENILE COURTS
Until the passing of the Children's Act of 1908, those aged under 16 were heard at the same courts as adults – fans of Charles Dickens may recall little Oliver being barely visible to the magistrate at the court hearing for pickpocketing – though in 1905 the first children's court had already been established at Birmingham. The 1908 Act brought juvenile courts into being and the records for these are held at county and borough record offices. However, lengthy closure periods have been imposed on these documents because of the youth of the defendants. Much of what applies to magistrates' courts applies here, though the sentencing will not be to adult prisons but other institutions. These later became youth courts, which dealt with those aged between 10 and 17 and could send the guilty to youth detention centres.

KING'S BENCH
The most senior court in the kingdom, which dealt with both criminal and civil cases, from the Middle Ages until 1875 was the

Court of King's Bench. Initially itinerant, as it travelled with the King, by 1422 it was settled in Westminster. It could hear cases in its own right and it could also supervise the lesser courts. It dealt with a wide range of offences from the relatively minor, such as assaults and brothel keeping, to riot and high treason. Many cases which came before it were from London, but also from the rest of the country and occasionally from the colonies, too.

King's Bench also dealt with treason trials (class KB8), and there is much information therein about the captured Jacobite rebels from 1715–16 and 1745–6. These include, for 1715, lists of almost 2,000 men who surrendered after the battle of Preston, giving name, parish and county of origin and occupation, sometimes company/troop and regiment if applicable; another list gives men's religions. There are also witness statements against some of the men who came to trial, which give details about their known involvement in the rebellion.

Archives are held at TNA. Indictment files for London and Middlesex from 1675 to 1844 are held in KB10; for the remainder of the country for the same dates, at KB11. Indexes can be found for London and Middlesex at IND1/6669–77 for 1673–1843 and at IND1/6680–4, and for the provinces from 1638 to 1704 and from 1765 to 1843. KB12 holds the papers for the country from 1845 to 1875. Depositions and witness statements can be found in class KB1 and 2; pleadings in KB31, sentences in KB21.

As with court records, these do not provide a text of what transpired in the actual trials. Sometimes newspapers give some commentary and information about the trials' general thrust, but without any significant detail.

CROWN AND MAGISTRATES' COURTS

In 1971 there was a dramatic revolution in the administration of justice in England and Wales in order to increase its efficiency. Gone were the quarter sessions and assizes and in came the magistrates' courts and Crown Courts, which replaced the two previous courts. Since 1956, this system had been operating in Liverpool and Manchester.

CROWN COURTS

These are the successors to the assize courts because they deal with that minority of serious crimes, such as murder, rape and robbery (about 5 per cent of the total), known as indictable offences. The defendant will first appear at a magistrates' court and then, if the evidence is compelling enough, they will be sent to a Crown Court, mirroring the earlier system where magistrates' courts could lead to a trial at an assize court. They are tried by a judge and jury of twelve, with a barrister representing the case for the prosecution and another for the defendant. There are a large number of such courts (seventy-eight in England and three in Wales). Some of the case files are held at TNA and these are indicated in brackets, with class number. In all cases, papers are closed for thirty years, though a Freedom of Information (FOI) request can be made. Most, though, should be held at local record offices.

The records fall into a number of categories. Those which should always survive are the Indictments. These give the defendant's name, sex, date of birth and whether bailed or not. They state the dates of trial and, if applicable, sentencing and conviction. The names of the court, judge, barristers and solicitors are listed. Finally the offence, plea and appeal details (stated grounds and date), if applicable, are given.

A selection of the case files survive, especially if the offence is particularly serious, if it is high-profile, involves a well-known individual or is of great public interest or other significance. These files include committal proceedings, court logs, police statements, a copy of the indictment, prosecution evidence, lists of witnesses, statements and depositions, list of exhibits used and photographs of the crime scene. However, transcripts of the trial are rarely kept unless it goes to appeal. They can be searched on the Discovery search engine at TNA's website by name of defendant. Court of Appeal registers for 1908–90 are at reference J81 at TNA; case papers are at J82 for 1945–93.

As an example, let's look at J207/89, Crown Court records for Maidstone in 1974. The first page gives the Statement of Offence; in the case of multiple offences by the same defendant, each may take up a separate page. In this example we see that the case is one of the Queen versus Jeremiah Jones and the 'Particulars of Offence' is that the latter, 'On the 25th day of August, 1974, at Margate in the County of Kent, stole a number of drinks and £4.00 in money belonging to Queen's Entertainment Centre (Southend) Ltd.' The date of the court hearing is 28 November 1974.

The next and, in this case, last page gives various useful details. Jeremiah Jones is stated as being male and born on 22 December 1922. He has been bailed and was committed for trial on 31 October 1974 and the hearing was on 2 and 3 June 1975. The judge was Recorder Wells and the court was Maidstone. Mr G Graeme was the prosecuting barrister and Mr S Evans for the defence, on legal aid. The crime was theft and the plea one of Not Guilty. The judge directed that a Not Guilty verdict be returned. Had it been otherwise, the sentence or court order would also be stated. It was noted that the defendant was discharged and that £60 of the allocated legal aid budget was to remain in the legal aid fund.

The records are in chronological order and there is no index, so you will need to know when and by which court the hearing took place. TNA's database, as with most assize records, cannot be searched by name of defendant.

MAGISTRATES' COURTS

Most defendants go before a magistrates' court, as they did prior to 1971 in many cases too, and there are a number of these throughout the country. These deal with lesser offences, known as summary offences, such as drunk and disorderly, vandalism, driving without a proper licence and so forth – in all, 95 per cent of cases. In 2015 there were 330 magistrates' courts in England and Wales. They are held before a judge or two to three (amateur) magistrates. Like their predecessors at quarter sessions, these were not qualified lawyers, as in the crown courts or assizes. Sentences offered are lesser, with a fine up to about £5,000 or a custodial sentence of up to six months. Community service sentences or suspended sentences can also be given out. Defendants sometimes elect to defend themselves or can call on their own or the duty solicitor. None of these court records, where they survive, are held in at TNA or LMA, but with the courts themselves, to whom research enquiries should be made. They include court registers and bail registers. Not all are likely to be kept indefinitely because of the sheer bulk of documentation that they represent.

Finally, don't forget the Court of Criminal Appeal, instituted in 1908 in order to prevent miscarriages of justice (the court of appeal for civil cases being founded in 1875). Used mostly in serious cases, an individual found guilty could then ask his solicitor to apply for an appeal hearing. This would be made up of a number of judges not present at the trial and barristers would appear for the defendant and for the Crown. Grounds for appeal were usually because there was fresh evidence or because the judge had allegedly misdirected the jury at the trial. Many appeals were turned down, but some could result in a lesser sentence or even an acquittal. For someone sentenced to death, an appeal was worth trying.

Court records are useful because they give concise facts about defendant, dates, offence and verdict, but they are limited and not easy to locate (except for the most heinous of offences) unless a rough date of the case's hearing is known. More details can be found in newspapers and for these see Chapter 5. It should also be borne in mind that for serious cases, before the 1970s, the initial hearing will be at a magistrates' or quarter sessions court, as evidence was presented there before the defendant was committed to trial at the assizes court, so records of both courts will need to be checked. These were often a few weeks or even months before the actual trial itself.

Chapter 2

OTHER CRIMINAL COURTS
IN BRITAIN

Apart from the courts which dealt with English criminal offences, there were a number of other court systems operating in Great Britain: military and naval, ecclesiastical and those in Scotland, Wales and other jurisdictions. Many had similar procedures, but with variations. We shall now turn to these.

ECCLESIASTICAL COURTS

The role of the church in our ancestors' lives up until the nineteenth century is difficult to overestimate and was on a scale unthinkable to most now living in more secular times. Much of this power in educational and legal affairs was transferred to the state in the nineteenth century. Jurisdiction was exercised through a variety of courts, well known to the family historian in name because of their dealings with probate to 1858, but they had other functions as well.

With the reintroduction of Christianity to England in AD 597, the church established itself slowly across the country. England was divided into two unequally sized provinces with a total of seventeen dioceses. These were the province of York with four dioceses, which included the northern counties of Northumberland, Durham, Yorkshire, Cumberland, Westmorland, Lancashire, Cheshire and Nottinghamshire. The larger province, however, was that of Canterbury, which included the remainder of the country. Each was headed by an archbishop and that of Canterbury was the senior of the two. Neither was head of the church in England; up to the Henrican Reformation of the sixteenth century this was the Pope, then the monarch thereafter when church and state fused and changed from Catholic to Protestant.

Beneath the rank of the province was the diocese, which was headed by a bishop. Diocese was not the same as county. Thus the diocese of Durham included Northumberland as well as Durham, and the diocese of Carlisle consisted of Cumberland and Westmorland. At the Reformation of the sixteenth century, six more dioceses were created but one, Westminster, only lasted a few years; a more permanent one was Chester, created in 1542 out of part of the diocese of Lichfield and it included Lancashire, Cheshire and part of Westmorland. Dioceses varied considerably in size and income. Durham was one of the richest in the eighteenth century, Carlisle and Rochester two of the poorest. Archbishops and bishops sat in the House of Lords and were important territorial and political figures with access to the monarch, as well as being key figures in the ecclesiastical world. They were appointed by the monarch, though the government took an increasing interest especially from the eighteenth century.

The next tier of administration was the archdeaconry; there were a number of these in each diocese, totalling fifty-eight in the country in the Middle Ages. Their number depended on size of diocese, and varied enormously, with Lincoln possessing eight, York five and Carlisle one. Archdeacons had to inspect the parishes in order to ensure that they were well run. Provinces, dioceses and archdeaconries all ran their own religious courts. There were also other ecclesiastical courts, known as peculiars, which were outside this system and only had very local jurisdiction.

Ordinary people came under the jurisdiction of these institutions. Church courts were established in Saxon times, but their role was more sharply defined under the Normans, clearly separating their and the Crown's judicial authority. Until 1858 (apart from a brief interlude under the Commonwealth of the 1650s), authority over probate was in the hands of the clerical courts. Secondly, these courts dealt with offences relating to religion and morals, if the two could be seen as separate, up to 1860.

These courts dealt with a variety of matters, though these tend to be less well known now. The church was concerned, naturally enough, with Christian morality and was empowered to deal with those who transgressed its boundaries. Because these courts dealt with sexual matters, such as adultery, fornication, divorce and incest, they have been named the bawdy courts. Other offences included slander, the refusal to pay tithes, non-attendance at church and Easter offerings. Witchcraft was dealt with by the church courts up to the sixteenth century when it became a civil criminal offence. Suits could be brought against clergymen, too, by both the laity and fellow clergy. Those damaging church property also fell under their orbit. It has been estimated that about a tenth of our medieval ancestors were brought before these courts.

Going before them was no laughing matter, however. Chaucer's archdeacon relished in the execution of the penal aspects of his role:

An erchedeken, a man of heigh degree
That boldely dide execucion,
In punisshinge of fournicacion,
Of Wicchecraft, and eek of bauderye,
Of diffamacioun and avoutrye.

Usually the initial step was for the churchwardens of the parish to inform the court of any parishioners who had caused offence. Either clergy or lay people would bring cases before the courts on these matters. A judge, who would be a senior churchman, would preside. Proceedings would be recorded in the Act Books, along with the results. Undisputed cases were resolved quickly but disputed ones involved the calling of advocates for both parties. If plenary procedure was followed, written pleas and statements were given. The plaintiff would provide the judge with his case for the judge to decide whether the court could deal with it. If so, he issued a citation on their behalf for the defendant to answer. This resulted in a number of statements for the defendant to answer. Witnesses would then make written statements against these points. Once the judge decided there was enough information from both sides, he would resolve the case and make a judgment. Costs would then be awarded. There was also summary court procedure, used in criminal cases only, when the evidence provided would be oral.

Those found guilty could be sentenced to a number of humiliating punishments. Public penance was a common sentence. They might have to stand in a designated public place for a set number of occasions, often on market days or on Sundays, and for a designated time, with a notice about their person stating their offence. Once this penance was completed, the offender would be advised to sin no more. The final deterrent to any proving obdurate was to threaten excommunication, though several warnings were given before so final a step was taken. In a world where Christianity was almost universal, this was no small threat.

Church court records are usually found in Act Books at the diocesan record office; those of Canterbury are found at Canterbury Cathedral Archives, those for York at the Borthwick Institute, and those of the dioceses either with the county record office or the cathedral itself. They tend to be less used than wills because they have not been indexed, as have most wills, and so searching for ancestors will be a lengthy task and quite possibly fruitless if your ancestors led sexually blameless lives. Of course, up to 1733 the documents will be in Latin, a further bar to some researchers. Act Books summarise a case to be taken before an ecclesiastical court. They give the depositions of witnesses, which include the witness' name, occupation, age, residence and perhaps information about their previous residence and work. There may also be cause papers, detailing arguments and evidence used in court. They were most active in the sixteenth and seventeenth centuries.

Some Act Books have been published, chiefly for the eleventh to the thirteenth centuries, in the *English Episcopal Acta* by Oxford University Press and the British Academy (see www.oup.co.uk for a list of those published). Some have also been published by county record societies and by the Selden Society.

Useful guides are C R Chapman, *Ecclesiastical Courts: Their Officials and Their Records* (1992), Ann Tarver, *Church Court Records* (1994) and Martin Ingram's *Church Courts: Sex and Marriage in England, 1570–1640* (1987).

Consistory Courts still exist and deal with offences committed by the clergy which are outside the usual array of criminal offences. They often deal with moral and religious issues which are of importance to the church but not to the state. Many of these records have been deposited at the diocesan record office, which is usually the CRO.

As an example, in 1490 William Cardell committed fornication with Alice Walsh and was subsequently brought before the archdeacon of Buckingham's court. In order to have the church's forgiveness he had to go around Hogston church in early spring on three Sundays dressed in only a shirt and barefoot and holding a candle. A humiliating and painful penance.

As the entry puts it:

Edlesburgh
Willelmus Cardell pro fornicacione cum quadam Agnete Walssh et candem impregnauit. Comparuit et fatetur articulum et fustigetur ter oer ecclesiam viz. quod transeat per tres dies Dominicos ante processionem nudis pedibus et capite discooperto in camisia cum candela in manu sua precij vnius oboli et in tercio die domincio offerat illiam candela ad imaginem beate Sante Marie in ecclesia parochialali ibidem. Prouiso quod perageret penitenciam tribus primus diebus dominicis in quadragesima iam proxime futura. Vocetur ad docendum de penitencia peracta. Peregit penitcenciam et dismissus est

More recent records are in English; as in the case of Parker the wife versus Parker the husband at the London Consistory Court on 26 November 1818. The opening papers read that Mr Parker was to answer Eliza Peters Washington Parker of the parish and county and diocese aforesaid, his lawful wife in a certain case of Divorce and deprived from bed board and mutual cohabitation by reason of cruelty and adultery by him the said Thomas John Parker, esq., committed and further to do and receive as unto law and justice shall appertain under pain of the law and contempt thereof at the promotion of the said Elizabeth Peters Washington Parker ...

When the cases proceed, lengthy witness statements give a great deal of information about the misbehaving husband and his mistress, as told from numerous viewpoints, which give an insight into part of their lives as seen by others. We don't, of course, learn much about the wronged party, who presumably was leading a blameless life whilst all this went on.

Furthermore, in the sixteenth and seventeenth centuries there was another church court, that of the High Commission, in operation in 1562–1641 and 1685–8. Court books, case papers and bonds are held for the archiepiscopal see of York at the Borthwick Institute and that for Canterbury at Canterbury Cathedral Archives.

WELSH COURTS

Wales is a principality which was ruled by England from the late thirteenth century. Although England and Wales were administratively linked in 1536, serious crimes in Wales were heard at the Great Sessions of Wales from 1542 to 1830, and thereafter at the Assizes in the four Welsh circuits as mentioned in the previous chapter. Monmouthshire, though, was deemed to be part of the Oxfordshire circuit. These courts could hear any type of crime but usually did not deal with petty crimes. Quarter sessions courts dealt with lesser offences, as was the case in England, and as in England, their records can be held in county record offices. Most of the judges were English and those who were Welsh mainly spoke English and so most of the records are in English. As with English Assize courts, they met twice a year in each county, usually in the spring and the autumn.

National Library of Wales. The Author

The National Library of Wales, at Aberystwyth, holds the Great Sessions archives, which include Crown and Gaol Books, listing those accused, the charge/s levied against them, their pleas, verdicts and sentences. Most of this information can be found on the Crime and Punishment section of the National Library of Wales website, www.llgc.org.uk/php_ffeiliau/sf_s.php.

Generally speaking, more records survive than for the English Assizes, but the survival rate is patchy. Examinations and depositions do not exist for many of the hearings in the English Assizes, but these records and those for recognisances often do for the Great Court of Sessions.

These records, from 1730 to 1830 are available for free on this website and can be searched by name. One such entry tells us that Morgan Evans of Llangurig, Montgomeryshire, yeoman, was accused of theft of household goods, including a brass pan, from Thomas Venables's house. Evans pleaded not guilty and the court's verdict was the same.

In the 1970s, as with England, the system of assizes and quarter sessions was replaced by Crown and magistrates' courts, as have been described in the previous chapter.

SCOTTISH COURTS

Unlike Wales, Scotland has always had its own judicial system, despite the Act of Union of 1707. Its principal court is the Court of Session. Its archives date from 1478 and can be found at the National Records of Scotland (NRS) in Edinburgh. It deals with most serious offences, such as murder.

The principal criminal court in Scotland is the High Court of Justiciary in Edinburgh. It deals with the most serious cases: murder, treason, heresy, counterfeiting and sexual crimes. It sits permanently in Edinburgh and travels on circuit throughout Scotland. It also acts as a court of appeal from criminal proceedings in sheriffs' courts. Its archives are held in the NRS.

There are several types of record. First there are the process or small papers, reference JC26. These include a copy of the indictment,

High Court of Justiciary, Edinburgh. The Author

setting out the charges against the defendant, depositions by witnesses, confession/s (if any), information concerning witnesses and jurors and any other evidence relevant to the crime in question. Then there are the summaries of proceedings, and for cases held in Edinburgh from 1576 onwards, these are in series JC6–9; for circuit cases from 1655, these are in JC10–14.

Books of adjournal are copies of indictments with brief summaries of trial proceedings; for Edinburgh cases from 1576 these are JC2–5; for circuit cases from 1890, they are in JC15. There are a few transcripts of trials from 1868 onward in series JC36. *Criminal Trials in Scotland, 1498–1624*, published in 1829–31; *Selected Justiciary Cases, 1624–1660*, published in 1953, 1972 and 1974; and *Records of the Proceedings of the Justiciary Court, Edinburgh, 1661–1678*, published in 1905. William Roughead, Edinburgh crime enthusiast, edited several famous Scottish trials in the *Notable British Trials*. More will be said about the latter in Chapter 6. In the NRS's public search room there are typescripts of trial indexes from 1611–31 and 1699–1720. Diet Books list Edinburgh trials from 1537 to 1828. Solemn Diet Books cover nineteenth-century cases.

Another important set of archives are those of the Lords Advocate's Department. These are the pre-recognition documents, references AD14–15. These are documents of written statements of witnesses about both the accused and the crime itself, which were created to put forward the case against the accused and most date from the nineteenth and twentieth centuries; there are few before 1812. The documents are closed for seventy-five years. It is worth noting that these records were created before the trial and in some cases there was no trial.

The AD records are similar to those witness statements taken by the police in England and Wales. As with these, not all the witnesses who give statements come before the court as witnesses for Crown or defence, so even if you know about the trial from other sources, it is still worth checking them. Even the statements of those witnesses who did give evidence at the trial are worth checking, for their comments at this stage are not necessarily used at the trial itself.

As an example, we can take the AD file for the John Donald Merrett case, where he was accused of shooting his mother and forging her cheques in 1926. Let us assume the reader is already familiar with the published trial transcript, as I was when I visited the NRS in 2014 to view the file. Some of the witnesses who had made statements were unknown to me as they were not called at the trial. These included Major Thomas Blackburn who was a friend of Merrett's mother, the victim. He gave a lot of information about meeting her and how he had tried to help the boy by interceding with the university authorities to get him a place there, how he knew of a misdemeanour of his when at school (claiming he had left school to stay with a friend Merrett was later found at the seaside) and then being disappointed at his being workshy at university.

Then there were statements by those witnesses who later gave evidence at the trial. Initially I ignored these, but on another visit decided to read through them. There was some similarity between the two sets, but there were also differences; and quite important additions, too. One of the witnesses referred to him as being 'not a talking boy'. Some of the nurses who had attended his mother before she died were critical of him, one stating 'I was struck by the callousness of Donald's behaviour in view of his mother's serious condition … I did not feel sure of him'. These comments about the behaviour and attitude of the murdered woman's son increase the likelihood that he did indeed murder her, as he was accused, and give further insights into his character that are found nowhere else.

Before the Union of 1707 there was a Scottish Privy Council (abolished in 1708) which often dealt with criminal cases. It usually concerned itself with cases where people of a high social standing were involved, but also with serious charges such as witchcraft and sedition. There is a thirty-five-volume register of cases from 1545 to 1691, which is indexed. Copies are available at the Britiish Library too.

Another aspect of the Privy Council was to hear pleas by the kinsmen and friends of people who had been kidnapped by the Barbary pirates from Algiers who often raided coastal villages in

Old Stirling Prison. The Author

Scotland and other parts of the British Isles and used their captives as slaves. Sailors might also be taken as slaves, too. The Privy Council often ordered collections to be made in parish churches for money to be gathered to pay ransoms. Names and other information about the kidnap victims feature in the Privy Council's archives; they might also feature in the kirk records, too.

Another court whose records are held at the NRS is the Admiralty Court, similar to the one based in London. In existence from 1557 to 1830, it handled crimes committed on the high seas. Series AC16 covers trial reports from 1705 to 1830; those from 1557–62 have been published.

There were other courts which once existed called franchise courts. These were held by local landowners, such as clan chiefs, regality, barony, stewartry and bailery. All apart from the barony courts were abolished in 1747 in order to weaken the power of the clans after the failure of the Jacobite Rebellion of 1745. These records are in class RH 11 at the NRS.

Most of those facing criminal charges in Scotland, though, go before the sheriffs' courts in the Scottish counties, and indeed those charged with serious charges will first appear before these courts, too, before being sent to the Court of Session or Court of Justiciary. These have existed since the early twelfth century, but in 1870 the thirty Scottish counties were dealt with by fifteen sheriffdoms. By 2015 there were thirty-nine, divided into six divisions. Sheriffs' courts deal with cases of theft and assaults, for example, but not murder, rape or treason. The courts deal with civil and well as criminal cases and until the nineteenth century the records of both were kept together. It should be noted that in Scotland, unlike England and Wales, a sheriff is a judge. The sheriff may make judgment alone or may work with a jury. They could sentence offenders to prison or fine them, but could not order anyone to suffer penal servitude, transportation or death.

Most of the sheriffs' court records are held at the NRS, though those for Kirkwall are at the Orkney Archives and those for Lerwick are at the Shetland Archives. The records include criminal court books, criminal registers and records, indictments and lists of juries. Most recently created records for these courts are not all kept, presumably on storage grounds, and what survives goes to the NRS after a twenty-five-year period.

Below the level of the sheriffs' courts are the justice of the peace courts, which were established in 1609, with quarter sessions dating from 1661. They were replaced in 1975 by district courts, but in 2007 the JPs were reconstituted. As with their English equivalents, the JPs are laymen whose work is overseen by a qualified lawyer. They deal with lesser offences and can only sentence the guilty to up to six months or issue them with a fine. As with the sheriffs' courts, archives are held both at local level and at the NRS.

Another local court was the burgh court, which tried minor offences in the royal burghs and these papers are either at the NRS or in local record offices. The least of the courts are the justices of the peace's courts. The records are held in local record offices.

Transportation records for those sentenced from the High Court from 1653 to 1853 can be found in series JC41. For witchcraft trials from 1572 to 1709 there are some indictments, summonses and

Rob Roy, Highland hero or robber. The Author

verdicts in series JC40. Witchcraft trials can also be found in local kirk sessions, in series CH at the NRS. Names of covenanters (religious dissidents) and others transported from 1679 to 1688 are in 115 bundles of lists of accused and depositions of prisoners and witnesses and can be found in series JC39. There are papers on the later Jacobite trials from 1748–9 in series JC7.

There are several differences between Scottish trials and those in England and Wales. First there are fifteen people in the jury, not twelve. Secondly, the opposing counsels do not make opening speeches before the examination and cross-examination of each side's witnesses begins, for it is believed that this will prejudice the jury for or against the defendant. Thirdly, the verdict of 'not proven' is permissible, meaning that the prosecution has not proved its case against the defendant but that they are probably guilty, as occurred in the cases of Madeline Smith in Glasgow in 1858 and John Merrett in Edinburgh in 1927.

Scottish church law system was different from that of England, both before and after the political Union of 1707. As with England, there were several layers of church courts. At the lowest level of the parish there was the kirk sessions made up of the minister and the kirk elders. They dealt with moral offences which included excessive drunkenness, slander, fornication, licencetiousness and such like. The sessions meetings minutes would record the name/s of the accused, their offence and their sentence. The next level was that of the presbytery court in which a number of parish elders and ministers would meet together to deal with witchcraft, excommunication and more serious cases of adultery and fornication if these two last had been referred upwards by the kirk sessions. They would detail offenders, their offences and their punishment. Then there were the kirk sessions which dealt with incest and disciplined immoral clergymen. The highest of the ecclesiastical courts in Scotland was the synod but its records are not useful for family historians. The archives for these courts, which withered away in the nineteenth century, are split between the NRS (in class CH2) and the county record offices.

ELSEWHERE IN BRITAIN

There are a number of other jurisdictions, each of which have their own system of courts. The court systems in Jersey and Guernsey are rather different to those in the remainder of the British Isles because of their French heritage. Records of Jersey courts are the Court de Samedi, which also included bankruptcy material (1618–1917) and the Court of Cattel, from 1504. Another criminal court is the Poursuite Criminelle Court, from 1797 onwards, which also dealt with inquests from 1806. Less serious offences were dealt with by the magistrates' court from 1854. These can be seen at Jersey Archives at St Helier. They are closed to researchers, however, for 100 years.

Although the Isle of Man has been subject to the Crown since 1765, it has maintained its own Parliament, laws and courts. Chief among these is the Manx High Court of Justice, but the lesser courts are the summary courts overseen by a bench of lay magistrates in the case of lesser crimes and the High Bailiff or their deputy and a jury in the case of major offences. There is also the Court of General Goal Delivery for the most serious of all criminal offences.

Records for courts are held at the Public Records of the Isle of Wight. They include Newport records of convictions from 1714 to 1833 and indictments from 1768 to 1836. There are petty session records for Newport from 1837 to 1919 (indexed 1837–88) and for Country from 1891 to 1957 (also indexed). Coroners' records from 1850–64 and 1886–1906 include names of the deceased, cause of death, place and ages, and are indexed. There are also records of prisoners and quarter session records held here.

THE HIGH COURT OF THE ADMIRALTY

This court dealt with offences committed on the High Seas in British ships or in British waters and on the Thames below London, from 1535 to 1835, these powers being granted by the Commissioners of Oyer and Terminer. Up to 1660 the court met at the Guildhall, London, or in Southwark; and thereafter at the Old Bailey. The court came to an end in 1834 and its powers shifted to the Old Bailey.

Until 1733 the records are all in Latin and legal script and often give fictitious details of defendants. Documents are held at TNA. An example of an indictment with comment on the result is as follows:

Admiralty of England
24th October 1826 Indicted and puts himself and Jury say guilty of manslaughter only, no goods. To be transported beyond the seas for the term of his natural life.

The jurors for our Lord the King upon their oaths present that Samuel Libbey late of London mariner not having the fear of God before his eyes but moved and seduced by the instigation of the Devil in the nineteenth day of September in the sixth year of the Reign of our Sovereign Lord George the Fourth by the Grace of God of the United Kingdom of Great Britain and Ireland, Defender of the Faith, with force and arms upon the high seas within the jurisdiction of the Admiralty of England that is to say about the distance of 600 leagues from the Island of Wahoo in parts beyond the seas in and upon one Thomas Taite in the peace of God and our said Lord the King and in and on board a certain ship called the Kent then and thus being feloniously wilfully and of his malice aforethought did make an assault and that the said Samuel Libbey with a certain knife made of iron and steel to the value of two pence which he in his right hand then and there had and held him the said Thomas Taite in and upon the right side of the body of him the said Thomas Taite did then and there feloniously wilfully and with malice aforethought strike, penetrate and stab and that the said Samuel Libbey by such striking penetrating and stabbing the said Thomas Taite with the said knife as aforesaid did then and there feloniously wilfully and of his malice aforethought give unto him the said Thomas Taite in and upon the said right side of the body of him the said Thomas Taite one mortal wound of the width of half an inch and the depth of five inches of which said mortal wound the said Thomas Taite did then and there die. And so the jurors aforesaid upon their oath aforesaid do say that the said Samuel Libbey hit the said Thomas Taite upon the high seas within the jurisdiction aforesaid in manner aforesaid feloniously wilfully and of his malice aforesaid did kill and murder against the peace of the said lord the King his Crown and Dignity.

COURTS MARTIAL

Since the seventeenth century Britain has had a standing army and a Navy in permanent existence, though at varying strengths, reaching maximum numbers during the world wars of the twentieth century. Many men did not want to be there, having been conscripted or joined as an alternative to hunger or, if convicted of crime, as an alternative to the punishment offered. Discipline had to be maintained against soldiers or others who disobeyed their superiors, especially in the relatively commonplace instances of plunder and desertion or, rarer, mutiny. Punishments, up to the end of the nineteenth century could include flogging, though this was unusual in the second half of the century and abolished in 1881, or in extreme cases, death by firing squad, though the latter was usually commuted as soldiers are expensive to train and equip so are not disposed of without good reason.

MILITARY

Courts martial records are held at TNA, as are the bulk of military and naval records. We'll take the army, the largest of the three services, first. There were three main types of courts martial: General courts martial, the army's highest tribunal which dealt with officers and, in serious cases, other ranks. In wartime, Field general courts martial were used which needed fewer officers present. They could impose the death penalty.

Lesser courts were the General regimental courts martial, termed district courts martial after 1829. They could not try officers or impose the death penalty. Registers of such for 1812–29 are at WO89 and from 1829 to 1971 at WO86 (for London cases 1865–75 use WO87 and for India 1878–1945, use WO 88). Information listed is basic.

Finally there were regimental courts martial for other ranks charged with petty offences. No records of such exist at TNA as returns were not sent to the Judge Advocate's Office. Some may survive at regimental museums. Registers of deserters from 1811 to 1852 can be found in WO25/2906–34; for captured deserters from 1813 to 1848, in WO25/2935–54 (indexed for 1813–33).

For the First and Second World Wars there will usually be reference on the individual's service record that the man was brought before a court martial and this should include a date of the event. This could be in the attestation papers or the pension file. In the case of Private John Christie, the latter documents his petty misdemeanours of being absent without leave and the minor punishment he was given. However, 300,000 men and 6,000 officers came before them during the First World War. The majority of court martials were for fairly trivial offences such as drunkenness and absence without leave (not desertion). Records of these rarely survive, however, though as with civilian crimes, the more serious the crime, the higher penalty, more ink, as well as perhaps blood, will have been spilt.

Registers of twentieth-century court martials for serious offences are in the series WO213; those covering the Second World War are numbers WO213/35–65. These ledgers are divided into Field and Military Courts Martial. The ledgers give basic details such as name, rank and regiment of the accused, location of trial (often only 'In Field'), name of offence and verdict. For the First World War, ledgers for men on service overseas can be found in WO90 and in WO92 for offences committed in Britain. For men accused of more serious offences in both wars, case papers can be seen in WO71 ns WO 93. The cases of the very small minority of men shot for offences can be read about in Julian Putkowski and Julian Sykes, *Shot at Dawn*, published in 1998. As ever, the higher the crime/penalty, the more information exists.

A couple of examples taken from WO213/6 are as follows. One of the cases held at Etaples on 15 October 1915 concerned Rifleman

Military Prison, Winchester. The author

44

C Parker, of the 9th battalion of the King's Royal Rifle Regiment. He was found guilty of being drunk and was given field punishment for twenty-one days. On the following day sapper A J Francis of the Royal Engineers was found guilty of disobedience and was given two months. Other punishments included loss of pay, discharge with ignominy and loss of rank.

More serious offences are the minority and are covered in more detail at WO71, 691–1001 covering the Second World War. These include trial transcripts and possibly additional evidence and photographs. However they are closed to public inspection and so a FOI enquiry would be needed to have any chance of seeing them.

The following court martial record comes from a hearing which took place on 24 June 1756:

> The Prisoner Phineas Goodhall Private Soldier in the Fiftieth Regiment brought before the Court and accused of Desertion.
>
> The Evidence given against him is as Follows:
>
> Lieutenant John Billings of the Fiftieth Regiment Deposes upon Oath that he knew the Prisoner Phineas Goodhall to be a Soldier in the Fiftieth Regiment and in the Grenadier Company and subsisted as usual that he saw him in Albany the 13 June 1756 with the Provincials with a firelock on his shoulder. He then immediately apprehended as a Deserter.
>
> Dennis Swiney Private Soldier in the Fiftieth Regiment and in the Grenadier Company being duly sworn deposes that he knew the Prisoner to be a Soldier in the above Regiment and Company and that when the Regiment lay last Summer in Camp Island near Boston the Prisoner had a Furloe for three or four days in order to visit his friends and that he went but never return'd.
>
> Lieutenant George Bartman of the Fiftieth Regiment deposes upon Oath that he remembers the Prisoner to be a Soldier in the Fiftieth Regiment and Grenadier Company and that he did duty as such that a few Days before the Regiment

march'd from Boston which was some time in June 1755 the Prisoner got a Furloe for two or three days and that he never return'd to the Regiment.

The Prisoner being put in his Defence says he was taken ill when he was on Furloe and that when he recover'd he did not know where to join the Regiment.

The Court having heard and examin'd the Information brought against the Prisoner together with what he had to offer in his own Defence, is of opinion that Phineas Goodhall Private Soldier in the Fiftieth Regiment is Guilty of the Desertion laid to his Charge and Doth therefore Adjudge that he suffer Death for the Same.

Bussell Chapman

Major of the 44th Regiment

This Court Martial was appointed of by his Excellency General Shirley

Richard Bowyer

Judge Advocate.

ROYAL NAVY

Likewise, Royal Navy records of courts martial are patchy in their survival, except for those coverings serious offences. ADM series 156 and 194 cover the period of the Second World War, with the latter series covering the Portsmouth and Plymouth divisions. Again, only basic details of each case are given. You should be able to find if your naval ancestor got himself into trouble by checking his personnel file if he served in one of the world wars. These will usually note the date and place of the court martial along with verdict and punishment.

In the case of Jack Alfred Field, his naval record for the First World War notes that he was discharged after punishment for desertion on 1 December 1919, having been previously arrested by the police for trespass in Newcastle. He had also been remanded on a naval warrant at Eastbourne and conveyed to Portsmouth on 10 March 1920, having escaped from the latter on 9 February 1920. No wonder his character was deemed 'indifferent'! Similarly Lieutenant Commander Ronald Chesney's personnel papers for the Second World War note a court martial at the war's end for theft and fraud, and this is particularly useful because the record of his court martial no longer survives. It reads:

> Court Martial held on 7th and 8th Nov. 1946 on charges of 1, Theft of car, 2, Fraudaulently obtaining a car, 3, Theft of Government Petrol, 4, Act to prej.[udice] etc. in not returning car, 5, Act to prej. Etc. in not returning the car, property of His Majesty. Charge 2 was found not proved, but remaining charges proved. Sentenced to four months imprisonment. The Board reviewed the case and decided not to interfere with the sentence.

It also notes that, on 24 April 1951 he was sentenced by a civil court to twelve months' imprisonment for smuggling bank notes and coffee beans.

A rather more complete court martial record file exists at ADM156/192 for Harry Green, Able Seaman. The initial sheet gives a basic overview of what happened, namely that Green, a sailor on board HMS *Irresistible*, had in 1905 been sentenced to eighteen months' hard labour in prison for striking a senior officer in the course of his duties. Green would be sent from the Mediterranean to England on HMS *London* to serve his sentence.

The following pages give more detail. There is a note from the Judge Advocate on 5 April 1905 that Green had not been tried in accordance with naval regulations and so as no new warrant for a court martial could be issued, the situation was unsatisfactory and so the sentence would have to be quashed. There are then the minutes of the proceedings, giving time, place and ship where it was held and a list of officers present at the hearing, all from different ships.

The Charge Sheet gives a report of the alleged misconduct. That is, Petty Officer William Till took the cell prisoners to the forecastle and ordered some of the other men to clear the forecastle for the prisoners. Apparently Green said, 'It is a f——g fine thing to have to clear the forecastle for prisoners'. Till then ordered Green to fall in on the quarter deck, which he did, but 'While waiting for the officer of the watch, Green suddenly made a rush at Till and struck him several times on the face with his clenched fist' before others could restrain him. Green pleaded guilty and all he could say in mitigation was that he had pleaded guilty to the charge.

Then there is the prisoner's statement:

> About 1.20 pm on the instant, I was lying on the Barbette, starboard side, asleep in the sun, when I was woken by someone saying, 'This is bloody sad'. I did not say a word until Petty Officer Till said to me, 'Fall in on the quarter deck'. I remarked, 'It is sad' and went aft in a dazed condition, as I had had my rum and had been sleeping in the sun, was not properly accountable for my actions. I do not remember striking Petty Officer Till, but do remember being charged with the offence. I am very penitent with regard to this occurrence, as I was trying to repair my character in the ship. And now throw myself on the mercy of the court.

Finally there are other sheets about Green's service in the Navy and other relevant details. The former include a list of ships he had served on and the ranks he had, together with his conduct and leave. There is also his date of birth, parish and county of origin, his former trade, his religion, whether he could swim (he could) or not and his date of volunteering. His height, hair and eye colour and any other distinguishing marks are noted. Finally we are told that the charge was dropped as his statement was apparently not accepted by the court as it would have upset the guilty plea and it should have been taken into account.

ROYAL AIR FORCE

As with the army, a personnel file will note whether an RAF ancestor had to stand before a court martial. Registers of courts martial are found in AIR21, listing name, rank, place of trial, nature of trial and verdict. There may be additional information in series AIR 18 covering a number of cases, and here far more information is available (trial transcripts, witness statements, photographs and so on). AIR 43 is a series giving comments about trials made by members of the Judge Advocate's department and are arranged chronologically, so may also be worth checking.

We have now looked at the formal records of the trial and, assuming there was a guilty verdict, the next step is to see whether anything can be found out about their punishment. Do not assume that the sentence given at the trial's end was in fact what happened to the defendant. Not everyone sentenced to death was executed (it was in fact a minority) and, just because a prison sentence of fifteen months was awarded, it is not certain that the defendant served fifteen months in prison.

Chapter 3

PUNISHMENT

If and when the defendant has been found guilty, what then? There was a variety of punishments open to the court, depending on the date. Historically these were whipping, a fine, transportation or execution (imprisonment for debtors); from the nineteenth century imprisonment was frequently made use of as the others, except fines, were abandoned and debtors were no longer gaoled. As noted already, sentencing and punishment were not always the same.

It is important to note that the defendant whose case is not dealt with relatively summarily at a magistrates' court will spend some time in prison prior to their trial. This is known as being held on remand and is requested by the police at the hearings at the lower court. The defendant then spends time in prison (for London prisoners this was often in Brixton Prison in the twentieth century) and is brought from his cells by prison officers for his hearings at the lesser court before the eventual trial at an Assizes or Crown Court. Their stay in prison could be several months as Assizes only had two sittings per year. John Haigh had over four months of imprisonment from his arrest on 28 February 1949 to his trial at Lewes in June of that year.

EXECUTIONS
Execution was a common sentence for those convicted and became more widespread in the eighteenth century when more offences were deemed capital ones. This meant death by hanging in public (and this included those found guilty of witchcraft who were not, contrary to popular opinion, burnt, though heretics were), with the

Old Dungeons, Yarmouth. Paul Lang's collection

possibility of being drawn and quartered. For noblemen death by beheading was their lot, as occurred to Lord Lovat, the last man to be legally beheaded (for treason) in Britain in 1747. Military offenders were often shot, as per Admiral Byng in 1757. The condemned would be transported through the streets to a place of execution and often made a confession before death. It was seen as a highly important piece of street theatre to emphasise the power of the state and the heinous nature of the crime for which death was the penalty. Up to 1827 prisoners could plead 'benefit of the clergy' if they could read and so be pardoned for the first offence by being branded on the thumb, so they could not use the same ploy twice, rather than being hung.

Executions were far fewer from the early nineteenth century as the number of offences punishable by death were rapidly reduced, leaving only treason and murder. In 1868 the last man to be hanged in public in Britain was Michael Barrett, a Fenian. From then on hangings took place within prisons and the most the public could see was the raising of a black flag and a notice plastered on the prison gates to denote that an execution had occurred. Capital punishment was suspended in 1965 and ended in 1969, though was still in theory possible until 1998.

Even in the heyday of capital punishment, relatively few of those found guilty of capital offences were actually executed. Of over 200 men held at York Castle in 1746 for high treason, having taken part in the Jacobite Rebellion of the previous year, only seventy-five were tried and of the seventy found guilty, twenty-three were executed, usually on the basis of being seen to have had a greater degree of guilt or because of their higher social status. Most of the remainder were transported or enlisted in the army; a few died in gaol or were pardoned or escaped. In 1716, of over 1,200 prisoners taken in rebellion, which was punishable by death, only 39 were executed in the north of England and 639 were transported. That having said, the Bloody Assize of 1685 resulted in about 300 executions and about 1,000 transportations.

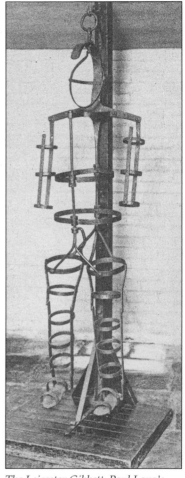

The Leicester Gibbett. Paul Lang's collection.

Financial papers of the sheriffs, responsible for the county gaol, often give an insight into the procedure, because they had to submit accounts of costs incurred for these executions. These records are held at TNA. For the years 1714–1832 they can be found at E370, for 1745–85 in T64, for 1733–1822 in T90 and for 1823–1959 in T207. Some of these have been published: in 1859–60 *Transactions of the Lancashire and Cheshire Antiquarian Society*, those for the

Plaque to victims at Dunblane Cathedral. The Author.

Lancashire sheriff for 1716 were published, though they say little about individual prisoners.

The Prison Service has been run by the Home Office, since 1877, and so their archives are held at TNA; they can be searched online for individual prisoners. PCOM series 8 and 9 deals with those condemned to death in the twentieth century and gives information about the last weeks of their lives between sentencing and death (or reprieve). They may include letters written to and from the prisoner to friends and relatives, reports by the prison's medical staff and references to last-minute efforts at a reprieve. They might list the prisoner's state of health and other physical details and often list his visitors. Item HO324/1 lists deaths in prison from 1834 to 1969 and many of these after 1868 will be of those executed.

In the case of John George Haigh, found guilty of the murder of Mrs Durand-Deacon in 1949, there was the possibility that Haigh was a schizophrenic, but following interviews with him, this was discounted. There was 'no evidence of genuine delusions or

John George Haigh, 1949. Author's collection

hallucinations', nor that he was 'mentally abnormal or irresponsible' despite his attempts to convince them so. The doctors concluded that he was:

> alert, attentive, calm and collected. His intelligence is good. He is adept in quickly inventing a statement to suit his own immediate advantage ... He shows no remorse ... his replies are generally intended to convince us that he is insane and irresponsible. He is quite unconcerned with the rights and feelings of others.

This led to a report being written to conclude that he was sane and so the Home Secretary could write 'The course of the law must take its place'.

The same file includes copies of letters written by Haigh, one being:

> Dearest Mum and Dad,
> ... other nations are more enlightened than we are. They don't hang people for their religious convictions. We on the other hand have not got past the days of beheading heretics. This case may be a wonderful day for England. It may make them realise that religious freedom is not yet complete. If so I shall go down in history as another martyr to my faith as great as Cranmer.
> Lots of love Sonnie.

These provide insights into the mind of the condemned man and also show how others viewed him.

PCOM files often give the cause of death and details of the execution. In the case of the executions of Jack Field and William Gray at Wandsworth in 1921, there are the exact times of death; 8 am on 4 February. In the case of Gray, we are told his sex, height, weight and other details that the executioner would need in order to estimate the drop required for the execution. Gray was described as being 'spare but muscular'. After death, the coroner examined him and found that there was 'dislocation between 1 inch and 2 inches cervical vertebrae and rupture of the spinal cord. Considerable laceration of the muscles on the side.' The file also gives details of the executioners and their assistants as well as a news cutting about the executions.

Minor offenders might be flogged in public, often on more than one occasion, and might spend time in the stocks, liable to public ridicule and a whole lot worse if they were unpopular. In the case of three men who were sentenced to such in 1755 for conspiracy in thefts in Deptford leading to others being hanged, one was killed

Stocks, Shoreditch. Paul Lang's collection

and two later died because of the hatred of the people against them. Generally speaking, though, little is said. Fines were another popular option, dating from before 1066 and still exist for lesser crimes as magistrates' courts routinely hand them out as sentences.

TRANSPORTATION

The bulk of documentation which survives about convicts is for those who were transported because this entailed a great deal of record keeping among many different people. From the early seventeenth century, with the growth of British colonies overseas, notably in what is now North America, but also in the West Indies, it was seen that these lands had the potential to be used as places for convicted criminals. Labour was scarce and manpower often welcomed. From 1615 to 1776 the Privy Council authorised this method of disposal of convicts. Prisoners could be shipped over once a contract had been entered into between the justices of the peace (then responsible for prisons) and merchants with ships at so much per convict. In 1716 Sir Thomas Johnson was paid 40 shillings per prisoner to be sent overseas.

Generally speaking there is relatively little information available about those sent to the Americas, partly because fewer were sent but also because the bureaucratic machinery which created so much paperwork in the nineteenth century and beyond did not exist. There are some useful parts of Ancestry which should be searched: Middlesex Convict Transportation contracts, 1682–1787 and the same for Dorset from 1724–91. These are searchable documents which list convicts to be transported by stated contractors; a date of the court's decision to award the said contracts is given, along with names of those to be transported, but very little about the individuals themselves.

The calendared Colonial Office Papers often list transportees, as below:

Mr Sec. Methuen to the Governor of Jamaica. Encloses list of rebel prisoners ordered to be transported to Jamaica, and requests lists of those rebel prisoners who have landed there. List of 47 rebel prisoners sent on board the Two Brothers, Capt. Edwd. Rathbon Commander, for Jamaica, in order of transportation. Leverpool, 26th April, 1716 …

After the American War of Independence began in 1775, prisoners were housed in prison hulks, old ships that were moored in the Thames or elsewhere. These vessels were usually moored off the coast. On Ancestry there are the hulk registers and letter books from 1802 to 1849. Searchable by name, these give prisoners' names, ages, offence, when and where the offence was committed, the sentence and the ship detained in. One example is John Lanchester, aged 22, found guilty of a felony on 20 April 1814 in Middlesex, sentenced to seven years' transportation and currently on the *Bellerphon*.

Transportation was resumed because of the overcrowding in the hulks. Convicts were then sent to Australia, the 'First Fleet' arriving in 1788, a practice which began to diminish in the 1850s and was ended in the following decade. In the 1830s there had been debate in Parliament as to whether transportation was too harsh or too lenient, with the result that those sentenced to seven years or less should serve their sentences elsewhere, in Britain, Bermuda or Gibraltar. Some were offered the opportunity to enlist in the armed forces if of the right age and in good health.

Transportees went to New South Wales until 1840, Van Dieman's Land (now Tasmania) until 1853, which roughly received 80,000 each and Western Australia, from 1850 until it ceased to receive them in 1868, about 9,800. Often men would be sent for a period of seven years but some were given longer sentences. Some returned to Britain thereafter but to return before the end of the sentence was to risk death until 1834 and then transportation for life. About 40,000 had been sent to the Americas and 162,000–170,000 convicts were sent to Australia. The lot of the latter has been well documented.

There are lists of those who were transported and these lists include names of those who were born and died en route, with dates (T46/22). Many of the documents concerning transportation can be searched on Ancestry. They include indexes of those transported on the First Fleet of 1787–8, on the Second Fleet of 1788–90 and on the Third Fleet of 1791. The information to be found about each convict is their name, the vessel they sailed on, the date of conviction, the date of the voyage, place of conviction and colony to which they were sent. An example would be John Smith, convicted on 11 August 1784 at Kingston upon Thames and sent on the *Scarborough* in February 1787 to New South Wales as part of the First Fleet. Lists of those sent on the fleets of 1791–1868 can also be searched and the information to be found is similar: name, where and when convicted, vessel's name, date sent, colony sent and term of transportation (usually seven or fourteen years or life).

On board ship, the convict may well have come under the notice of the ship's surgeon and in 1858–67 the latter seem to have kept lists of convicts with their level of education noted, whether it was nil, day school or Sunday school.

Once in Australia, the authorities insisted on a great deal of paperwork about the new arrivals during their life there. These include muster rolls of convicts in New South Wales and Tasmania and those for 1806–49 can be searched on Ancestry. These were in effect mini-censuses, but taken more regularly; in New South Wales in 1806, 1811, 1822, 1823–5 and in 1837 and in Tasmania in 1811, 1823, 1825, 1830, 1832, 1833, 1835, 1846, 1847 and 1849. The following example gives an idea of the kind of detail they provide: the 1837 muster rolls show Alfred Brown, born in about 1793, convicted in Sussex and who arrived in New South Wales aboard the *Malabar* in 1819.

Other searchable listings on Ancestry include the Australian Convict indents, 1788–1842, settler and convict lists, 1787–1834, convict muster rolls, 1790–1849 and the 1828 New South Wales census. Most provide the same information – name, age, vessel sailed on, when and where arrived and date and place of conviction. Settler and convict lists also provide occupation of the said individual and the census gives their address. Those who went on to commit further offences might be found in the Gaol Description and Entrance Books for 1818–1930, which can be searched by name to find the date of admission into gaol and the name of that gaol, as well as the usual details (name, birthplace, arrival year and vessel travelled in).

There are also documents available on Ancestry concerning convicts' applications to marry from 1826 to 1851. One example is that of Richard Swaine, aged 25 and Mary Connor, aged 26, both of whom had been sentenced to seven years and who had been sent out on the *Coromandel* and *City of Edinburgh* ships respectively. Their request was refused on 16 April 1829 because no one of the name of Mary Connor had travelled on the said *City of Edinburgh*.

Many convicts were pardoned before their sentence ended. On Ancestry can be found Convict Registers of Conditional and Absolute Pardons, 1788–1870. One example is Francis Smith, born in 1815, aged 36 and conditionally pardoned at Sydney on 1 February 1851. He had travelled to Australia on the *Lady Nugent*, arriving in 1835 after having been sentenced at Hertfordshire on 7 April 1834. Physical descriptions are often included and details of their offence, especially towards the end of the period in question.

There were also lists of pardons and tickets of leave from 1834 to 1859, which only give a convict's name, the ship travelled on, his parish of origin, date of sentence and of arrival in Australia, and sentence in years.

Certificates of freedom for 1810–14 and 1827–67 can also be searched on Ancestry. These provide a wealth of useful biographical information on the subjects in question. William Oates had been sentenced to seven years' transportation for burglary at Lancaster on 20 October 1828 and had been sent on the *Marquis of Huntley* to arrive in Australia in 1830. He had grey eyes, a sallow complexion and was five feet and two and a half inches tall. He was sent to Norfolk Island on 18 November 1833 and was set free on 16 December 1844. It was noted that he was nearly blind in his right eye.

To take an example of a man bound for Australia. James Burgess was found guilty of being involved in the Gold Bullion Robbery of 1855, an audacious and initially successful train robbery. He was sentenced to fourteen years' transportation at the Old Bailey. Transportation records reveal that he was put on board the ship *The Edwin Fox*, which arrived in Western Australia on 21 October 1858. He was given a ticket of leave on 14 July 1859, which essentially meant that he was on probation. He could work anywhere in the colony but could not leave without a magistrate's permission and had to report to the law periodically. He was given a conditional pardon on 21 March 1862, so was able to travel unimpeded but was not allowed to return to Britain until his fourteen years were over. After 1862 he no longer appears on the transportation records.

PRISON

Imprisonment was relatively rare until the nineteenth century as a form of punishment, except for debtors. Prisons were there to hold prisoners before trials and then to hold them before execution, transportation or other punishment. They were not there to keep people in for a sentence of time and so were rarely purpose-built, often being in castles located in county towns. There were other buildings, too. These were termed houses of correction or bridewells, established by the JPs and some of them later became county prisons, as with the case of Wakefield. Records of prisons up to the early nineteenth century and of the JPs' dealings with them can be found in the quarter session records at CROs.

With the abolition of the death sentence for many offences from the 1820s onwards, and with the decline of transportation as a means of punishment in the middle of the same century, another way had to be found to deal with those found guilty of crime. Fines were still often imposed for relatively trivial offences, such as being drunk in charge of a horse and cart, or for first-time offences, but these were inadequate for the more serious crimes. Imprisonment seemed to be the answer and gaols were purpose built in the nineteenth century (with a general reduction in crime in the 1920s–1930s several were closed). Prison sentences began to be the norm. They were also seen as places of rehabilitation where prisoners could be educated and trained to lead useful lives on leaving prison, as well as being places where they paid for their crimes by the loss of liberty and often had to undergo hard labour, which was termed penal servitude and this latter tough option (usually allocated to persistent offenders) was in force until 1948. In prison, prisoners could be birched for breaking prison rules until the 1960s. Prisoners would not necessarily be sent to the nearest prison from the place where sentenced; in 1951 Ronald Chesney was sentenced for smuggling at Lewes Court but spent his sentence in Wandsworth Prison in south London, not Lewes Prison.

The key records for prisons are, from the family historian's point of view, prison registers, for they list the prisoners in chronological order of arrival. Newcomers' details are entered into a register. These are sparse: name, physical description, level of education, religion, date of entry, sentence, length and date of departure. They are rarely indexed by name. These are often held at the county record office for the county that the prison is located in. Thus the London Metropolitan Archives holds the registers for Wormwood Scrubs, Wandsworth and Holloway Prisons, and for the Feltham Young

Aylesbury Convict Prison. Paul Lang's collection

Offenders' Institute. Wakefield Archives hold the registers for Wakefield Prison. Some registers are still held at the prisons in question; those for Brixton and Pentonville Prisons are still there; contact with the governor should be made in these instances. There will also be closure dates for these sensitive registers; often of up to a century, because of the data protection rights of former convicts and so access may not be permitted. However in many places a researcher can pay the staff to make a search for an individual on their behalf.

Many of the prisoners at Wandsworth were photographed and the photographs of those for 1872–3 who were sentenced to one month or more have survived and are held at the National Archives. They can be identified by TNA's database and so can be viewed. There is also information accompanying the pictures: name of prisoner, description (height and hair colour), education (this could be on a scale of 1, meaning illiterate, to 6 denoting a clerk, or whether they could read, write and do mathematics; or not as the case may have been), date and place of birth, crime and sentence, place of conviction and intended residence after expiry of sentence.

One such prisoner was Joseph Charman, aged 12, who had received a six-week sentence with hard labour for the theft of a fowl. He was also ordered later to serve five years on a reformatory ship, *Cornwall*, moored off Purfleet.

A number of prison registers can be viewed online on Ancestry. These include the West Yorkshire Prison Records, 1801–1914, and can be searched by name. These give name, date and place of committal, offence, sentence, education, religion, occupation, birthplace, age and physical description. One example is as follows. John Oates was committed on 13 March 1885 at Batley Borough for using obscene language. He had been found guilty and had been given the option of paying a fine of 20s 7d or spending seven days in prison. He had had no education and was aged 67, with brown hair and was five feet four and three-quarters inches high. He was a labourer, born in Mirfield, was an Anglican and had two previous convictions. His nose had been broken, he had small burn scars on the left groin and left hip. His third finger was crooked.

Then there are the Dorchester Prison Admission Registers from 1782 to 1901, also available on Ancestry. The information required was similar to that wanted by the West Yorkshire authorities. The same site has the Bedfordshire Gaol Index from 1770 to 1882.

A number of registers of prisoners can be found on FindmyPast, for the period 1770–1935. These are registers of convicts in prison hulks, 1818–31, after trial calendars of prisoners, 1855–1931, the Home Office calendars of prisoners, 1868–1929, petitions from prisoners, 1817–58, Metropolitan Police registers of habitual criminals, 1903–14, judges' reports on criminals, 1784–1830, and an index to criminal petitions, 1797–1853.

Other useful websites for prisoners are as follows: www. yorkcastleprison.org.uk (5,000 convicted eighteenth-century prisoners in York Castle), http://tinyurl.com/p5g5fpd (prisoners in the Warwickshire county gaols of Warwick, Birmingham and Coventry from 1800 to 1900), http://apps.bedfordshire.gov.uk/grd (details of 35,000 Bedfordshire prisoners from 1801 to 1901), www. rootsweb.ancestry.com/~engchs/prison.html (inmates at Chester

Gaol, 1810–16), www.staffsnameindexes.org.uk (calendar of Staffordshire prisoners from 1779 to 1880) and www.genuki.org.uk/big/wal/CGN/CGNCriminals.html (Cardiganshire Constabulary's register of criminals, 1897–1933).

Some other prisoners can be found on registers available on Ancestry. These are those for the King's Bench and Fleet prisons; discharge and prisoner lists from 1734 to 1842. These were for insolvent debtors and the registers list names of those there who beg relief, together with the date. Marshalsea prison committal and discharge books from 1811 to 1842 can also be searched, and they list names, dates of admission and discharge.

Irish prison registers from 1790 to 1924 are online at FindmyPast. Prison registers for Scottish prisons, generally dating from the nineteenth and twentieth centuries, are mostly held at the NRS in series HH21. They provide details of the trial and sentencing, and for the prisoner, place of birth, occupation, age, height and religion. For some there are photographs of prisoners and there are indexes to a few of the registers. Administrative records, series HH12, may refer to individuals and there are a small number of files relating to prisoners in series HH15. Records for sheriffs' courts' prisons are split between the NRS and local records; these are mostly for the eighteenth and nineteenth centuries.

It should be noted that there is very little in prison records about the day-to-day existence of the inmates in prisons. Other prison archives, such as the minutes of the management may shed a light on general matters of policy and practice in the prison, but are unlikely to refer to individual prisoners unless they have behaved in a particularly heinous manner while inside. As with school logbooks and minute books of workhouses, they should give an insight into administration in the prison. It may be worthwhile checking any published histories of the prison or any memoirs of former inmates for further information about a prisoner's life there. These are discussed in Chapter 6.

Prison records are often found among quarter sessions records, for until 1877 the counties were responsible for local prisons. They can include Bread Accounts, which exist for Middlesex's prisons in sixty-four books from 1750 to 1782, listing poor prisoners who were entitled to free bread. Likewise for that county are beer books, listing prisoners in receipt of beer.

Please note that a prisoner might not spend all his/her prison career in the same institution, especially if his sentence was a lengthy one. Those sentenced to short periods in gaol, perhaps weeks or months, would generally spend the duration in one prison. John Christie spent his ten weeks of a three-month sentence for theft in 1921 in Manchester Prison. But those given more than a year in gaol might well be moved about. Donald Hume, imprisoned first on remand and then as a sentence for being found guilty as an accessory to murder, spent 1949–50 in Brixton and Wormwood Scrubs Prisons in west London, then 1950–4 in Wakefield Prison and then 1954–8 in Dartmoor Prison. Prison registers give dates of arrival/departure into each place.

A more liberal penal code began to be introduced in the nineteenth century. Prisoners could earn a reprieve and so be released from prison earlier than the date set out in their sentence. A licence could be granted by the Home Office to prisoners. Those for female prisoners from 1853–71 and 1883–7 can be searched on line at Ancestry. They give an impressive amount of information about the prisoner and her prison career, as can be seen from the following example:

Order of a Licence to a Convict made under the statutes 16 and 17 Vict. C.99, s9 and 27 and 28 Vict. C.47, s4.

Whitehall 31 day of January 1865

Her Majesty is graciously pleased to grant to Jane Simpson, who was convicted of Receiving at the Sessions of the Peace holden for the county of Lancaster at Preston on the 3rd day of August 1860 and was then and there sentenced to be kept in penal servitude for the term of six years, and is now confined in the Fulham Refuge. Her Royal Licence to be at large from the day of his liberation under this Order during the remaining period of his said term of penal servitude, the said Jane Simpson shall before the expiration of the said Term be convicted of some indictable offence within the United Kingdom, in which case such licence will be immediately forfeited by law, or unless it shall please Her majesty sooner to revoke or later such licence.

This licence is given subject to the conditions enclosed upon the same, upon the Breach of any of which it will be liable to be revoked whether such Breach is followed by a Conviction or not.

And Her Majesty hereby orders that the said Jane Simpson be set at liberty within thirty days from the date of this order.

The document, which is several pages long, then goes on to state the 'Particulars of Periods of Confinement and Conduct while in Convict Prisons'. That was that she was at Millibank Prison for thirteen months and twenty-five days, at Brixton for two months and four days and then at Fulham for thirty-three months. Whilst in the prisons, her general Character and Conduct was deemed 'Good', and her progress at school was judged 'Very Satisfactory' at Millibank and Fulham and 'Tolerable' at Brixton. In prison she had worked at needlework and had also been employed in the laundry at Fulham.

There were then the dates of her imprisonment; at Preston on 8 August 1860; then at Lancaster Castle from 8 August to 17 December 1860; then at Millibank from 17 December 1860 to 11 February 1862; at Brixton from 11 February to 15 April 1862; and finally at Fulham, being discharged on 8 February 1865 with her destination then being Preston.

The originals can be seen at the TNA in PCOM4 (index at PCOM6). For male convicts the records are not online but can be viewed at TNA in the series PCOM3 for 1853–87, arranged chronologically, and there are indexes for 1853–81 at PCOM 6.

Appeals for mercy were often sent to the Secretaries of State or, after 1784, to the Home Office, on the behalf of prisoners facing the death penalty or other sentences in the hope that the sentence would be reduced to transportation or a pardon. Petitioners would often cite the prisoner's youth or extreme age, suggest that the crime occurred due to provocation, or they might empathise with the plight of relatives who would suffer unduly if their main breadwinner was no more. Previous good character could also be stressed. Thus these petitions provide much information about the prisoner and his/her family, though of course these papers will take care to show them in the best possible light in order to have the maximum chance of success, so may not be wholly accurate.

For pre-1784 petitions, State Papers at TNA will need to be checked; most of the references to these are indexed and can be located online; the documents may then need to be checked on microfilm at TNA. Pardons on condition of being transported from 1654 to 1717 are entered on the Patent Rolls, C66, but others are to be found in the Criminal Entry Books SP44 (up to 1782).

Separate series relating to such applications begin in 1784. Judges' reports in HO47 covering 1784–1830 contain information compiled by judges at the end of Assizes and Old Bailey sessions. They list those convicted of capital offences with recommendations for pardons. They often provide a great deal of information about the trial witnesses and the judge's comments on their evidence and honesty. They may also refer to the defendant and include character references. Other letters from judges appear in HO6, which are circuit letters from judges. They can give additional information about the defendant, their crime and whether they should be treated with mercy.

Petitions for mercy can be found in HO17 for 1819–40 and at HO18 for 1839–54. They give name of prisoner, date and place of trial, offence and result of petition. Formal records of pardon can be found in HO13 (1782–1849) and in HO15 for 1850–71. Those for 1887–1960 are at HO188 and give far more information about the case and why a pardon was granted. Each of these volumes is indexed.

One such petition with accompanying papers concerns Robert Farquhar, in 1822. The main document is a letter from the prisoner. It reads as follows:

Petition of Robert Farquhar of Peter Culter, Aberdeen
That your Petitioner was indicted before the Lords Commissioners of Justiciary for *two different crimes of assault*, at their last Spring Circuit held at Aberdeen, along with a person of the name of Lobban then residing at Feddy in the parish of Skene. That it is with deep contrition and a heart full of penitence for said crimes, that your Petitioner with every dutiful and humble submission now approaches your Majesty, in the confidence that you will not disdain the application of an individual who has unfortunately being involved in the present instance through the instigation of Labbon, a man evidence of a depraved and malicious disposition. That your Petitioner did not at his trial put their lordships to any additional trouble as he voluntarily confessed his guilt, and his lordship (Lord Gillies) was pleased, after consideration, to sentence your Petitioner to *nine* months imprisonment, and Labbon to twelve in the House of Correction, Aberdeen, in which the Petitioner has remained a Prisoner ever since, having undergone six months of his punishment.

That your Petitioner humbly begs leave to state that he rents a farm of *Fifty Pounds* sterling of yearly rent, from Mr Gemmell of Countesswells and that he has a wife with three helpless children. That during the confinement the Petitioner's wife has been under the necessity of hireing at extravagant wages, persons to manage the cultivation and improvement of his farm, and the cutting down his crop this season, whilst under the peculiar circumstances of the times bears hard on your petitioner's fate.

That your Petitioner has always hitherto bore amongst

society an irreproachable character and rather of a docile than of an obstreperous disposition; and that no individual in his, or the neighbouring part of Skene, can in any ways impute to him a contrary behaviour as is attested by the ministers and elders of the united parishes of Peterculter and Skene which is hitherto produced.

That your Petitioner therefore with humble submission, prays for your Majesty's clemency on his behalf, and that after you deliberate on said certificates, with the additional recommendations of the respectable individuals who have voluntarily come forward on the present occasion to support your Petitioner your Majesty may be inclined to mitigate his punishment by allowing his liberty, particularly when you consider that this is your Petitioner's first transgression, and he hopes and sincerely trusts will be his last. And as in duty bound your Petitioner shall every Pray.

Robert Farquhar

The elders and clergy wrote three separate notes, all to be found together with the said petition. One states that Farquhar had lived in the parish for several years and his young wife and three helpless children were 'in indigent circumstances'. Another noted that he had 'lived in the parish five or six years … always maintained a good character and behaved … in a decent and becoming manner'. The third noted that Farquhar was 'a good natured industrious young man', that they had 'never knew or heard of anything unbecoming his peaceful demeanour until the present' and that his offence had been at the instigation of another. The fact that his wife and children were suffering because of his imprisonment was also mentioned.

After all that, there was the Home Secretary's concise remark, 'Let the Law take its Course'. Although the petition was of no use to Robert Farquhar, the petition should be of immense value to family historians.

Justice could be merciful, of course, and with a petition in favour of Robert Hampton, found guilty at the Surrey General Quarter

Sessions in 1789 of acquiring goods illegally by using counterfeit messages and sentenced to be transported for seven years, is a letter from Joseph Mawbey, chairman of said court. It read as follows:

> The Prisoner is a very young man and may, therefore, by Penitence, still make a useful member of society:- but the persons with whom he is connected, appear to me to be so profligate and abandoned, that, unless he be removed from *them*, there will be every Reason to expect a Repetition of Criminality – If His Majesty in his great Clemency, should be graciously pleased to pardon him, on Condition of his serving the *East India Company* in some of their settlements, I am humbly of opinion, that the Ends of Public Justice may be answered, and the prisoner restored in a useful manner to society.

MENTAL HEALTH

Some prisoners, increasingly from the early nineteenth century, were deemed to be insane and so were incarcerated elsewhere. This was especially the case following the formulation of the MacNaghten Rules. These had been devised following the murder of Edward Drummond, Robert Peel's secretary in 1843, by the apparently deranged Daniel MacNaghten. There was no doubt that MacNaghten was guilty, but it was also apparent that he did not know what he was doing whilst killing his victim. The MacNaghten Rules, which persisted until the late 1950s in Britain, stated that if it could be proved that a defendant either did not know what they were doing or, if they did, did not know that what they were doing was wrong, they would be deemed 'guilty but insane' and therefore not face the death penalty but a period of time in Broadmoor Lunatic Asylum from 1863 or Ashworth and Rampton from the twentieth century onwards. Before 1843, insanity was no defence; as John Bellingham found after shooting Spencer Perceval MP dead in 1812; he was hanged.

In 1863 Broadmoor Institute was opened near Crowthorne in Berkshire. From its inception until the early twenty-first century women were admitted as well as men (carefully segregated of course). However not all those there are convicted of any crime. Numbers there have varied over time. Patients are there until they are deemed cured, when they may be released outright or may be sent to a less secure institution or may be sent to a prison. Some have died there. Another similar institution, Rampton, was established in 1912 in Nottinghamshire and another, Ashworth, on Merseyside in the 1970s. The criminal insane can also be sent to

'Hanwell' Asylum. Paul Lang's collection

more general mental hospitals, once called asylums in the nineteenth century, though this is often when they have been to Broadmoor and are deemed a lower risk.

For the family historian, mental health institutions have established lengthy closure periods over all records about specific individuals. The closure period is usually at least a century after the death of the inmate/patient. Some records are available, however. Those for Broadmoor are at Berkshire Record Office and asylum records are usually found in the appropriate county record office (LMA for Colney Hatch and Middlesex for example). For instance, the Broadmoor patients' journal includes poetry and short stories by patients, as well as comments on social life and sporting/recreational/social and educational activities on offer. Those for the 1980s include poetry by Reginald Kray, though it is unlikely his verses would have caused the then poet laureate to fear for his eminence. Contemporary brochures aimed at inmates or/and visitors can also provide insights in the regime at the institution in question, and should be accessible to researchers.

Often when patients left they were sent to another mental hospital, one less secure, but from where it was hoped that the patient could, after further treatment, be set free. One such institution near London was the County Asylum at Southall after 1831 and another was Colney Hatch from 1851. Registers of patients are held at the London Metropolitan Archives and are closed for 100 years.

There are a number of online sources at Ancestry which assist in the tracking down of criminals who were suffering from mental health problems. These include the Lunacy Patients' Admission Registers from 1846 to 1912. These list name, whether the patient is a private one or a pauper, the date of admission and whether they have been deemed insane or not. The Criminal Lunatic Registers for 1820–43 include patients at Bethlem Hospital from 1823 to 1843 and those at licensed asylums for 1800–39. The information is sparse, giving name, date and place of sentencing and offence. Benjamin Smith was found guilty of assault at Worcester Assizes in August 1839, for instance.

The Criminal Lunacy Warrant and Entry Books for England and Wales from 1882 to 1898 are another searchable source on Ancestry. They give name, offence, date and place of sentencing, sentence, former prison and present location. One example is that of Alfred John Smith, found guilty of larceny at Birmingham City Sessions on 3 March 1892. Sentenced to eight months' hard labour at Warwick Prison, on 3 June he was certified insane and removed to Hatton County Lunatic Asylum until further order had been issued or until his sentence expired.

TNA also holds files about the criminal insane. These included MH51; Lunacy Commission and Board of Control's files from 1798–1971. This correspondence and papers includes law officers' opinions, orders for the removal of lunatics from asylums and gaol returns of insane prisoners. HO343 are a series of Home Office mental patients' files from 1927 to 1986. The Home Office is responsible for the transfer of prisoners from conventional prisons to mental hospitals; serial killer Peter Sutcliffe being controversially rehoused in Broadmoor in 1984 from HMP Parkhurst, for example. The file for Donald Hume concerns correspondence and newspaper files about the return in the 1970s of this British killer from a Swiss prison to Broadmoor because during his incarceration he had become mentally unwell and the Swiss system did not have anywhere designed for that type of person. The Home Office was reluctant to accept such a dangerous man but eventually had no option. There are also letters to and from the police as to whether Hume could be tried, if released, for bank robberies committed in Britain prior to the murder he committed in Switzerland. There are also reports about his mental state from Swiss psychiatrists (these are closed at time of writing in 2016). MH103 includes files where people are transferred from hospitals into institutions for the criminally insane.

On the subject of hospitals, it may be worth remembering the archives of general (non-psychiatric) ones. People injured by criminals as a result of assaults will usually end up in hospital to be treated for their wounds. How long were they there, which did they attend and how were they treated? Hospital archives may well have the answer. The main class of archives here are the hospital registers which are created to record basic details about each patient so treated. These are arranged chronologically and are hefty document registers, not always indexed and rarely available online. The main points to note about them are that they are almost always closed for 100 years, are usually to be found in the appropriate county or borough record office and not all survive. The website Hosprec is the best finding aid to locate what survives and where it can be seen.

OTHER PUNISHMENTS
There is generally little more to state about punishments such as probation, fines or flogging. These will be simply stated in the court register with the amount imposed. Sometimes the prisoner was given the option of a fine or a short gaol sentence, usually for a fairly minor offence. If your ancestor was subject to such, you could try reading general accounts of this type of punishment to gain a relevant insight for a punishment which leaves very little imprint on the records but not necessarily on the offender or his pocket.

YOUNG OFFENDERS
With 7 as the minimum age of criminal responsibility, young offenders were dealt with no differently than adults if 14 or older, until the nineteenth century, and it was not unknown (though rare) for youngsters to be hanged if charged and found guilty of a capital offence (it was only in 1908 that 16 was the minimum age for a hanging and so in 1921 15-year-old Harold Jones escaped with his life after murdering two little children in his home town in Wales). Yet it was increasingly realised that it was in the best interests of all that they be dealt with differently and be kept apart from hardened adult prisoners who could inculcate further criminal habits into them.

In 1825 a prison hulk, the *Eurydale* was set aside for offenders under 16 and in 1838 the first prison for youths was established on the Isle of Wight – Parkhurst. It housed 300 lads and the plan was to train and educate them so to reform them and then to transport them to New Zealand or to Australia, the latter with a conditional pardon. Conditions were strict and were criticised by prison reformers. It was closed in 1864 and by then other institutions had been established throughout the country.

Reformatories were begun in 1854 for young criminals aged between 14 and 16 and for those aged under 14 who were felt liable to become criminals (sometimes vagrants). There were also industrial/training schools. These latter were to instruct children in useful, if menial trades, so that they could earn their livings by legal means when they left. In 1924 about 15,000 children, mostly boys, attended these.

Both these types of institution were replaced in 1933 by approved schools for the under-17s and there were borstals from 1902 to 1983 for young offenders aged 16–21. Remand homes were established in 1901. The Children's Act of 1932 made capital punishment only for those aged 18 or over (so that in 1953 the 17-year-old Derek Bentley could not hang for shooting dead PC Miles in Croydon). These establishments were renamed in the 1980s as Youth Custody Centres and Young Offender Institutes.

Records of inmates in reformatories in West Yorkshire from 1856 to 1914 can be searched by name in Ancestry. There are three main types of record for such institutions: commitment books, admissions and discharges. They certainly contain a wealth of information. We'll take them one at a time.

Commitment books are organised by the institution. They give date of admission, name and date of birth of inmate. Then there are the physical details: height, weight, hair and eye colour and any distinguishing marks. It is stated whether the child is illegitimate or not. The school attended, if any, is declared, along with whether the inmate can read and/or write and do ciphers. Parents' names are included. If the child had a prior occupation and residence, that will be noted. Then there is the offence charged with, the date and place of conviction and the names of the committing magistrates. The sentence will be given, and the inmate's 'Previous Character'.

One such young reprobate was John Smith, born on 25 August 1872 and admitted to the Shadwell Children's Centre on 23 June 1882. He was three feet and nine inches tall and weighed three stone and six pounds. The colour of his hair and eyes went unrecorded. He was born to married parents but it was unknown whether he had been to school previously. His father was dead and his mother was in Armley Prison. His previous occupation and residence were unstated. His offence was 'Wandering and not having any visible means of subsistence' (perhaps not surprising as his sole parent was in prison). He had been committed at Leeds on 23 June 1882 by Robert Addyman and George Emyrs. He was sentenced to six years and two months so would be there until 25 August 1888 and was placed in a school on 9 October 1882.

Then there are the admission books, giving name, age, place of birth, height, weight, eye and hair colour and other marks. The nature of the offence and the place and date of committal are stated, as are the names of the magistrates. Education and previous occupation are noted.

Richard Saxton was one such admitted on 19 March 1888, aged 15. He had been born in Whitby, was four feet eight inches tall with hazel eyes and weighed 100 pounds. His offence was stealing coals at Whitby and he had been sentenced there on 28 February 1888 by Mr J C Walker and J Furnival, to four years. Although he had attended St John's school, Whitby, he was unable to read, write or cipher, yet his intelligence was rated 'Fair'. He had been employed by Mr Hartland, a Whitby farmer, and also had hawked crabs with his father, William, a fish hawker. He lived at Church Street, Whitby. It was commented that his father was 'Bad. Encourages his children to beg and steal. A brother in penal servitude and one in Castle Howard Reformatory.'

Finally, there are the discharge books. Apart from the inevitable name, address and admission and discharge dates, there are also comments about the career following discharge, showing that the former criminal was having his progress monitored by the authorities. One such was B Stephenson, admitted to East Moor

Home on 30 May 1904 and discharged on licence on 13 October 1908. He was 'to reside with his parents at 8 Westfield, South Church, Bishop's Auckland'. His first year's report in 1908 was a letter from his mother to say that he had begun work at a blacksmith's shop at Eldon Colliery at 6 Rose Mount, South Church. The second year's, on 10 October 1909, was that he was still employed by the same blacksmith. The third year's in 1910 was that he was a pony driver at Adelaide Colliery in Bishop Auckland. Apparently his conduct there was 'satisfactory' and he then lived at 6 Rose Mount, Bishop Auckland.

As with records of adult prisons and asylums, records of juvenile institutions are held at CROs, based on their location. There are lengthy closure periods on these documents in order to protect those whose names are included.

SCHOOLS

We should remember that since time immemorial pupils were chastised, often most severely, for real or imagined misdemeanours committed whilst in school, or merely on the whim of teachers or prefects who enjoyed such pastimes. This heinous behaviour was abolished in 1986, but for many children it was a regular part of school life. Such admonishments were commonplace in homes, too, but in schools this began to be recorded by the beginning of the twentieth century. Prior to this such punishments would have gone unrecorded.

They were listed in the ominously titled 'Punishment Books' which are sometimes found amongst school or local authority education archives. These will be found in CROs or at the school itself, as is the case with one of the proofreaders of this book, who was caned at his prep school.

These books were used in order to regulate physical chastisement in schools, often the cane, from 1905 to the abolition of such punishment in 1986. They are arranged chronologically, giving pupil's name, reason for punishment, the number of strokes and who dealt these out. There may be additional comments about the pupil, such as 'persistent troublemaker' or 'warned twice'. Instances of corporal punishment decline over time, so that by the 1970s its use was very infrequent. The books only survive for a handful of schools and are usually closed for long periods of time, often for 100 years, in order to protect confidentiality under data protection legislation. Furthermore, only a small proportion of pupils are listed here, and often the same ones appear several times.

Let us take an example from Little Ealing Junior School:

Punishment date	Name	Age	Standard	Offence
11.9.06	Ivy Farrow	12	IV	Disobedience

Amount of Punishment	Remarks	Signature of Teacher
2 strokes		W Montgomery

School logbooks rarely mention individuals, but occasionally may refer to pupils being expelled or dealt with for persistent bad behaviour, and logbooks should be found with the school archives in the CRO or borough record office.

Another well-known institution in the nineteenth and early twentieth centuries was the workhouse. These institutions had their own rules, especially where the activity of the inmates was concerned. Often able-bodied inmates were obliged to work for their otherwise free board and lodgings. If they did not do so they could be punished and the surviving workhouse archives may well list offenders, with dates and punishments doled out.

Records of punishment add to the detail known about a particular criminal, but as ever it is worth studying the context of the criminal's experience by reading around the subject if at all possible.

Chapter 4

POLICE RECORDS

We now turn to those who were responsible for the apprehension of criminals and the maintenance of the rule of law and order. This book is not concerned with the police per se (*Tracing Your Police Ancestors* by Stephen Wade in the Pen and Sword series is recommended for those whose ancestors served in police forces), but, rather, with those whom they pursued. However, the records created by the police are important for they often deal with the criminals and their victims. The police are those who investigate crimes, arrest suspects, gather evidence, interview witnesses and hold suspects until they are sent to prison on remand pending trial or release.

For centuries the chief agents for the apprehension for criminals were the parish constables, aided and abetted in towns and cities by night watchmen. The former were unpaid amateurs who served for a year only and who had to arrest criminals and either convey them to a magistrate or to a lock-up or other place of detention for temporary housing. They have often been derided for inefficiency and incompetence, but this stereotype has been challenged in more recent decades. The only records they left behind them were constables' accounts where they itemised the expenses that they had incurred in the course of their duties. Even these rarely survive, but when they do they exist among parish archives of the parish that they served and so will usually be found in county record offices. These accounts, though, may well record payments for taking suspects to gaol and similar, but rarely mention malefactors by name and so are of limited interest to those researching their criminal ancestors.

Old Police Lock Up, Gnosall. Paul Lang's collection

In 1829 the Metropolitan Police was established in London, and extended to cover Middlesex and those parts of Essex, Hertfordshire, Kent and Surrey which were adjacent to the capital, in 1839. London was divided into twenty-two divisions, each of which was separately administered, with a Commissioner in overall charge, answerable to the Home Secretary. This was the best financed force in the country and developed many specialist services. In 1835 the Municipal Corporations Act enabled the 178 boroughs of England and Wales to establish watch committees and appoint constables. The 1839 County Police Act allowed the counties to form police forces, if they so wished, and over the next decade about half of the fifty-six counties did so. It was only the 1856 County and Borough Police Act which made police forces in localities compulsory. The Metropolitan Police were, until 1999, under the control of the Home Secretary, but the other forces were administered by Standing Joint Committees, made up of local councillors and magistrates.

There were, then, myriad police forces all over the country, of varying sizes. There was also the Thames River Police and the various police forces employed by the numerous railway companies. The City of London also had a police force entirely independent of the Metropolitan Police. Sometimes a county force and a borough force would both have a station in the same town. Oxford and Cambridge universities had their own police forces founded in the early nineteenth centuries prior to the publicly funded forces. Often more than one force might investigate a crime – in 1920 men from the Metropolitan Police, the Eastbourne Constabulary and the East Sussex Constabulary played their role in the search for Irene Munro's killers. The killing took place just within the boundaries of East Sussex's jurisdiction, but the nearest police station was that of the Eastbourne Force, and as was often the case, Scotland Yard had to be called in to provide expertise.

Over the next century or so, there was a trend to amalgamate smaller forces to create fewer but larger (and it was alleged, more efficient) police forces. There had been legislation to enable this as far back as 1840. In 1888 the Local Government Act abolished police forces in boroughs where the population was under 10,000. In 1946 the Police Act led to the abolition of forty-five non-county borough forces. Between 1964 and 1969 the number of police forces fell from 117 to forty-nine and the 1974 Local Government Act reduced them to forty-three. Meanwhile the railway police forces merged to become the British Transport Police following nationalisation.

In Scotland, between 1800 and 1832, a dozen large towns and cities established their own police forces. In 1857 there was a Police Act which made police forces in Scottish counties and burghs obligatory, creating numerous forces, as in England and Wales. In 1950 there were thirty-three forces, and as in the case of England and Wales they became more centralised as time went on; twenty-two forces in 1968 and eight in 1975. In 2013 Police Scotland became the single police force in Scotland and the second largest police force in the UK (London's Metropolitan Police being the biggest).

As with any institution, the police forces created records of their activities as they progressed. These records include those of crimes investigated. The majority of these cases are investigated by the detective force. Whilst some records are ephemeral, such as policemen's notebooks, disposed of after completion, others are kept. Many of these survive and can be viewed.

There are numerous types of record that, during the course of investigations into criminal activity, the police create. Foremost among these are witness statements. The police ask questions of witnesses and anyone who can make a contribution to the investigation. These can include the next of kin and friends of the victim, their colleagues and their neighbours. Often hundreds, even thousands, of statements are taken. Infamously, the West Yorkshire Police Force accumulated masses of papers, which were poorly organised, during the Yorkshire Ripper Case of 1975–81.

STATEMENTS

A witness statement is a statement made by the witness to the police, beginning with their name, age, address and occupation. It is initially written down as manuscript and initialled by the witness and police officer to mark it as being a true record. It is dated. Often the statements, if deemed of importance, will be typed up and so are far easier to read. These are also more likely to be kept. The statements will be a brief narrative of what the witness saw and it might include reported conversation. These should help throw a light on the criminal and on the victim and their life and their relationships as these may have had a bearing on the case. Those who make statements will include suspects and perhaps the individual who is charged with the crime.

To give two examples of the insights into the character of murder victim and a man accused of her death, the following are taken from the National Archives file MEPO3/279 into the murder of Irene Munro, a 17-year-old typist, at Eastbourne in August 1920.

We shall take a statement about a victim first.

Statement of Ada Marian Beasley, age 17 years, living at 30a Finsborough Road, South Kensington, S.W. with mother who is living apart from her husband who carries on a fishmonger's

PC Thomas Ledger, 1953. Author's collection

Business at 63 Ifield Road, South Kensington, who saith: −

I am a shorthand typist employed by Messrs Bastin and Reffell, 329 High Holborn, Hotel and Hydro Agents, and have been there as such for past 2½ years.

I know the girl Irene Munro of 3 Manson Place, Queensgate South Kensington. She has been a friend of mine for past 6 years. I first met her at William Street Central School, West Kensington. We both attended this school until March 1918. She then found employment as a shorthand typist at Thierry's, Regent Street. She remained there about a year and then found another situation with Messrs Maxwell, Wright and Co., Regent Street, W. I know she was employed there definitely until 2 weeks ago.

From March 1918 until the beginning of March 1920, Rene Munro and I met about once a week. We never had any male associates up to that time … [There follows an account of the girls' romantic associations.]

About the end of June or the beginning of July 1920, I saw Rene at her office. I told her of my trouble [a sexual assault] … and she then said she had some trouble. I asked her what it was, but she refused to tell me, as it was not only her secret. From her conversation I gathered that it was a love affair as I remarked to her, 'What is it respecting a boy?'. She replied 'Well, what else would it be'. Nobody in her office overheard this conversation as we were alone …

Rene was a girl of lively disposition. She was not a flirt, neither was she fast. She was romantic in her ideas. She occasionally compiled verses, was fond of reading high class books, and seeing good scenery.

Then we have a statement about one of the two suspects, a young man by the name of William Thomas Gray.

Statement of Minie Hird, 156 Longstone Road, Eastbourne, who saith: –

I know William Gray. I first knew him when he came home in soldier's clothes and he used to go with Lily Anderson to whom he is now married. I was introduced to him by Doris Fox, 2 years ago this August; I was in London a year and this was before I went to London. I was about 16 then. About 4 or 5 months after I was introduced by Doris Fox. She and I went for a walk with him. This was in the evening about dusk. I think he had just got married; we all three went to Beachy Head and sat on the grass. I was on the outside, Doris next and Gray the other side of Doris. Doris got up and went to look over the cliffs and Gray moved over to me. He put his hand on my chest and pushed me down and said 'I haven't brought you up here for nothing'. I said 'I'm a respectable girl'. He said 'I would like to push you over the cliff'. This was because I would not submit to him. I got up and walked home and left him with Doris … I have seen Gray with girls occasionally since he has been married.

I have spoken to girls about him and they say he is no good
...

Sometime in August, one Wednesday night, Gladys Fielder and I were out together and when passing the Hippodrome we met Gray and Field. Gladys spoke to Field, I walked on and [he] overtook me immediately afterwards. When Gray tried to take a liberty with me I told him he was a married man and his place was with his wife. He said that he was not a married man but I told him he was.

These two statements, were, incidentally, never produced in court, but shed a great deal of additional light on the accused and the victim. Irene seems less the 'silly young woman' or being immoral as she is often portrayed in books. Gray, on the other hand, has his reputation even further diminished as he comes across as a rapist as well as a murderer. They may have been ultimately irrelevant in the conviction of the accused, because statements about previous offences, real and reported, cannot be made by the prosecution in court, but for the family historian are invaluable because we learn a lot more about both individuals.

Additional statements are sometimes made by witnesses if they recall more information or if the police think that they might know more than they first claimed. Often these are straightforward enough and simply more information is provided. Some statements are of more importance than others, with some being very peripheral indeed. For example in missing person cases, there are often hundreds of sightings reported and the majority of witnesses are mistaken. Those who report the discovery of the corpse in a murder case are of prime importance, of course.

Suspects often change their stories in order to produce one that is more believable than the last and will help them convince the police of their innocence. Which version, if any, is correct, is another matter. In 1939 William Thomas Butler was interviewed about the murder of a Surbiton jeweller, Ernest Key. At first he denied all involvement in the crime and alleged his injuries were the result of an unrelated accident. Evidence suggested he was at the scene of the crime, though. He was made aware of this and then made another statement, claiming that he had been the driver employed by the murderous thieves and had been given some of the proceeds of crime as a payment. Finally he made another claim that he had been at the jeweller's and had stabbed the elderly man to death, but it had been an act of self-defence on the young man's part. It is often said that statements of the accused more closely resemble reality as more are made. Some are often a mix of truth and fiction – Donald Hume, in 1949, later said that he invented a tale to clear himself of the crime but included reality where he knew the police could prove it and lied when he knew the police could not corroborate it. He then went onto make another statement, following conviction on a lesser charge, implicating a third party in the murder.

Statements may conflict with one another. Witnesses may give different versions of key dialogue or may not agree as to the exact timing of events in the case. They may give different versions as to personalities involved. They may not know enough of a relative's private life and may believe that someone is entirely respectable, whereas friends and associates have rather more accurate knowledge. Some of these statements may be later made in court, but many may not be, and even if the same witness does appear in court, not all of their statement may be made there.

Not all statements survive, however. In some instances all the witness statements have been weeded and so no longer exist. Why this is so for some cases and not others is impossible to know, but it probably does not suggest anything sinister, merely a haphazard method of record disposal.

REPORTS OF POLICE OFFICERS
The core document, however, is that made by the chief inspector in charge of the case. This is in the form of a report for his superior, to summarise the case and the evidence against the individual charged with the crime, if one is known. It will be a chronological record of the crime and will cite witness statements. This provides a conclusion

to the police investigation, and emphasises which of the evidence in the case is the most important. The officer will also usually make statements in the same format as witnesses, too.

The following example concerns a criminal who had committed two murders in London in 1954 and the report made when his corpse was found in Germany:

On the morning of 16 February, Kriminal Kommissar Erwin Kunn of the Cologne Police was informed of a discovery made by a retired postman in a stretch of woodland 25 yards from the Military Ring Strasse and 150 yards from Durenerstrasse on the north side of the city towards Ehrenfeld. He went to the scene and later made the following report:

'There I saw the body of a man since identified as John Donald Milner / Chesney / Merrett. The body was on its back. The right arm was stretched out level with the shoulder. The left arm was lying alongside the torso with the hand about level with the upper thigh. He was dressed in an overcoat of grey/white colour, three buttons of this coat were done up. The lower part of the coat was thrown back on both sides up to the level of the upper thigh. The body lay with the buttocks upon the rear part of the waistcoat.

'The pistol lay on the right leg of the body and had been fired, but there was no trace of blood on it. A hat was lying a few inches from the left of the body, and the inner part of it showed splashes of blood and parts of the skull driven outwards. On the left near part of the hat was a hole about 1cm in size.

'Milner / Chesney was wearing grey leather gloves. There was splashes of blood on the left trouser leg from the knees upwards to the level of the outer end of the upper thigh, some of which was as big as a farthing. To the left and right of the buttons of the coat there were splashes of blood which had partly run off. Some of these splashes were about the size of a shilling. There was also blood on the face.

'In addition to the overcoat Milner / Chesney was wearing a steel blue suit with a peacock serge pattern, and knitted waist coat and shirt with red and white stripes, a red tie and a grey woollen scarf. There were numerous spots of blood on the collar of the shirt and the rear part of the woollen scarf, caused by the blood flowing from the mouth. This was clearly a case of suicide.

'Examination of the pistol showed it contained a spent cartridge, but the magazine was empty … in my opinion, death had taken place about seven or eight hours earlier'.

On Chesney's person and in his luggage was clothing, but there were other items, too. These included 11 indecent sketches, a cardboard file with papers concerning The Anglo-German Export Company, a copy of the News of the World for the 14th, pipes and cigar cases. More sinister were the two white towels, both soiled with blood. The only cash was 10.8 deutschmarks; a far cry from the 600 which a witness claimed he had seen him with on the previous day. There was also a note, 'Everything I possess belongs to Miss Sonia Winnikes, 51 Josef Strasse, Duren. Signed John Donald Milner'.

MISCELLANEOUS

Previous criminal convictions of various parties (defendants, victims and witnesses) in the case are usually flagged up in police records, giving date and place of crime and conviction and these can lead to additional sources of information. Kathleen Maloney, a murder victim at 10 Rillington Place, had an extensive record of minor crime – theft, soliciting, assaulting police officers, loitering in various towns and cities. This police record then allows a researcher to check newspaper, prison and magistrates' court records for those localities in question and for those dates.

Medical reports made by psychiatrists and prison doctors can usually be found as the suspect/s are questioned about their medical history, both mental and physical. These can be quite detailed, though are often based on the suspect's own testimony. This is especially the case when defendants allege that they are suffering from mental illness or have family members who died in asylums or suffered mentally.

In the case of a murder, there should be a report made by the pathologist who carried out the post-mortem. These will be in severely scientific language, will be comprehensive and could be quite graphic. There may also be photographs of the crime scene which were never made public in the newspapers. These can be very shocking as they can include close-up photographs of the wounds inflicted and of the victim's face; they may include photographs of vital clues or of bloodstained rooms. They are deeply unpleasant to look at, but anyone interested in the case may well have to steel themselves and recall the fictional American private eye Philip Marlowe's dictum about mean streets being trod by those who are not themselves mean.

Scene of the Crime. Author's collection.

In an unsolved murder, in which the case is not closed for many decades afterwards, there may be additional letters, perhaps some anonymous, in which suggestions, often quite wild, are made about the possible perpetrator. For eighteen years after the murder of Vera Page in Notting Hill in 1931 there were letters received at Scotland Yard suggesting the culpability of various people as well as noting clues that the police should follow up. Often these concerned people that the writer had a grudge against, such as an estranged husband in one woman's case or an unpopular brother-in-law in another's. Letters from amateur sleuths and even spiritualists are not uncommon.

Recent police files will be closed to the public, or at least parts of them will be. This is especially so if the case is unsolved and if there have been fresh developments in subsequent years (for example, another witness coming forward or a new investigation). The definition of 'recent', incidentally, can mean the 1940s as well as more recent cases such as that of the murder of Sandra Rivett in 1974. Freedom of Information requests can be of use in some instances. A little more of a file that was partially open, about a murder in 1949, was recently reopened via a FOI request, so it is worth trying. In some cases, parts of the file may still be inaccessible, however.

Metropolitan Police files are held at TNA and can be frustratingly incomplete; but those of other forces seem even more incomplete (the Centre for Buckinghamshire Studies does not have any case files at all). Provincial police force records are held at the appropriate county or borough archives, where they have not remained at the police headquarters in question. Record office websites should be checked to see what the place holds. Cumbria Archive service has some case files from the Cumberland and Westmorland Constabulary including those for murder, fraud, burglary, treason, bomb throwing and on escaped prisoners. These are mostly closed for seventy-six years after the final date of the documents in the files. The same archive service also has photograph albums of prisoners from 1880 to 1910 from the Kendal Borough Police force. West Yorkshire Archive Service also holds numerous 'mug shots' of those convicted by the local forces from the early twentieth century, including one of the young John Christie in 1921, convicted of theft of cheques and postal orders. However, as with the Metropolitan Police, most surviving police archives focus on personnel, police stations and equipment. Archives of the university police forces for the nineteenth and early twentieth centuries are held in the principal university library (and include details of arrests – of students and non-students).

There are many types of police records which should be relevant to those researching criminal ancestors. They do not exist in all instances and some may still be in police hands. Some often only exist for a few years or decades and all concern the routine handling of prisoners. They include charge books, descriptions of person books, indexes of habitual criminals, prisoner reception and property books, crime registers, cell books, lists of prisoners out on licence and even photograph albums of prisoners. These records will help flesh out what happened to your criminal ancestor and when, in his or her dealings with the police. In all instances it is best to contact the CRO, or failing that the appropriate police authority.

There can be useful correspondence about miscreants, too. The London Metropolitan Archives has the archives of the City of London police (no connection with the Met). On 21 July 1882, the parish of Brighton contacted them about a man they wished to speak to and the letter read:

Sir –
We hold a warrant for the apprehension of the Rev. Thomas John Bailey for deserting his wife. We are informed he is connected with some office (loan or otherwise) in the City and it has been suggested to us that it might be the firm of Messrs Bailey and Co., 21 St. Bride's Street EC. Will you kindly allow your officers to make enquiries if he should be apprehended I would come for him at once upon precept of a telegram. He is a member of the Oxford and Cambridge Club. St. James' Square, **Pic**cadilly, is well known at Westminster Police and the Criterion restaurant.
Your obedient servant
E.J.Pearce, Warrant Officer.

Registers can be useful summaries. At TNA are the registers of Murder and Manslaughter, five volumes covering 1891–1958. They are arranged chronologically and for each instance give the date, place of offence, name of deceased and name of individual charged (not necessarily convicted) if known. This basic information can be useful for leading to other sources.

Many records simply do not exist. Amalgamations of police forces has not helped the preservation of archives and as recently as 1989 most were still police property. Donald Rumbelow, a one-time City of London police officer and crime author, records that, when document store rooms were full, an officer would be detailed to make room for new ones by just throwing some of the older files out without any method or order or selection. Sometimes police officers take files home on retirement for private study and these may then be lost forever. Even when records do survive, they may be heavily weeded. For example, in the Vera Page case, 1,000 witness statements were taken but all these are now long gone. Often papers are destroyed after they have been used in court. The numerous Criminal Record Office files, once of great use to serving officers in checking records of suspects, are now almost all gone, too. In part all this was because police records were not given the same importance by their creators or archivists that local government or church records were. The many amalgamations of forces as noted above has also led to the destruction of older records.

There were or are a number of other police forces. The Royal Irish Constabulary was the police force for Ireland until its disbandment with the establishment of the Irish Free State in 1922. Their archives are held at TNA. Apart from personnel files, some papers cover offences they dealt with. These are CO904 and 906 for 1905–22, covering disorders and attacks on officers. The force's role against violence between 1916 and 1922 is to be found in WO35. The police forces created by the railway companies were amalgamated on nationalisation to become the British Transport Police in 1947 and archives are held at Transport House, London.

There are also a number of police museums – in London,

Manchester, Chelmsford and Tetbury to name a handful. These are open to the public, often by appointment. They focus on the police officers themselves, their equipment and their methods, so are of obvious interest to those with police ancestors. Yet they may be of interest to this book's readers for they sometimes show mock-ups of police stations, prisoners' exercise yards and cells, or even be located in former police stations, which will give an insight into where your ancestor spent some of their time after arrest.

When a criminal ancestor is identified, recourse should always be made to the archives of the police force/s which dealt with him or her. The more serious or important the case, the more surviving material there should be. The same dictum applies to victims, too, though there will be less, especially if the victim was killed, for all the evidence will have to have been supplied by those known to them.

Chapter 5

NEWSPAPERS

Since the seventeenth century, Britons have read or listened to news being read from printed sheets of paper appearing at regular intervals. From 1702 there were daily newspapers (two or four sides of one sheet of unillustrated paper) and as time progressed these became lengthier and more numerous. Most were published in London but in the eighteenth century a healthy regional press sprang up – though it was not until the nineteenth century that these newspapers focused on local news rather than just regurgitating national and international news from other papers. Newspapers were there to inform but also to make profits and they concentrated on stories that would interest the readers, especially if those stories could be continued in several issues. Perhaps the three main topics were the activities of the great and good, war and crime. 'If it bleeds, it leads' is a famous saying of the newspaper industry; crime has always had a prominent place in newspapers and the bloodier the better, as far as the newspapers were concerned. The Jack the Ripper murders of 1888 gave the press a field day – the unknown killer's alias being very probably the invention of a journalist.

National newspapers, most of which are daily, report crime. This includes the major cases of murder, treason, bank robbery, significant fraud cases, kidnapping, arson on a major scale, political crimes, sexual offences and so on. But they often report on smaller scale assaults and burglaries as well. If the case involved a well-known individual the national press would probably also **pic**k it up. Some of the reporting may well be on a smaller scale than a local newspaper would employ. For instance in 1937 *The Times* devoted examined her, and found a rather severe scalp wound on the left side of the head, and the wound had the appearance of having been caused by a fall. There was a large quantity of blood in the kitchen, where it occurred. There was no other injury, and that one was caused by her falling against something. Deceased had been under his care for some time past, and he had known her for the past 20 years. She was suffering from an advanced state of chronic Bright's disease, and there was generally a tendency in such cases to fits. He was of the opinion that she had had a fit, and that, with cerebral hemorrhage, was the cause of death.

The Coroner having summed up, the jury returned a verdict of death from natural causes, in accordance with the medical testimony.

AFTER THE HOLIDAY— THE DOCTOR?

Force and not mere weight should be considered in most matters, especially in regard to the food consumed during the holidays. It is not a bit of use to take the children to the seaside, and let them revel in the sunshine, play on the sands, paddle and bathe, if you will allow them at the same time to derange their digestions. Now, sensible mothers, just reflect for a moment. Is it better to avoid digestive troubles and medicines, or to spend a long time with the latter when the holidays are over? The answer is obvious. Very well, then. Do not load up your children's delicate young stomachs with an excessive quantity of meat and starchy foods. Give them something that will feed and nourish, and not overtax the digestive organs. What is there, you say, which answers this purpose? Well, we are going to recommend Nature's food—the little Greek currant. That is the very best form of diet for children, because the dried Currant is pure grape sugar, Nature's most powerful and easily assimilated food. Currants feed and build up the body. It does not matter whether they are eaten raw or cooked—Currants are equally beneficial.

THE KING OF SPAIN AT DOVER.

The King and Queen of Spain arrived at Dover on Saturday, from Calais, by the turbine "Riviera."

Whilst the passengers were disembarking, the Spanish Ambassador went on board, and was received by their Majesties. Mr. F. W. Prescott, Spanish Consul, also conversed with the King and Queen, who later entered the

NEW MACHINE GUNS.

Machine guns are much in favour just now, says the "Army and Navy Gazette," and this year's patterns are a great improvement on former types as regards lightness, a quality which enables them to be carried up into the front fighting line. The machine guns on tripod mountings are now nearly as handy as the "portable" type, which has only a prop under the muzzle, and their shooting is far more accurate. The portable type has accordingly been practically dropped, except for cavalry. The new maxim weighs only 78lb., without shield, and the new Schwarzlose only about 70lb. The latter has a knuckle-jointed breech action, a type which is coming into favour in place of the straight bolt. Great things are expected of the Maag barrel-cooler. This is a water jacket with external radiator and internal air tubes, through which air is sucked at each shot by the action of the muzzle blast. It is stated that this prevents the water from boiling during rapid fire, avoiding the formation of visible steam, and the necessity for replenishing the water-jacket.

MONEY DUE TO SOLDIERS.

It has been notified by the Transvaal Post-office that various sums of money are standing to the credit of soldiers who at one time had deposits in the Post-office Savings Bank of the Transvaal. Officers commanding units are to forward to command headquarters the names of any soldiers who are still in possession of a Transvaal Post-office Savings Bank book, with a view to the recovery of any sums due, irrespective of the fact that the soldier believes his balance to have been exhausted. The sums now due are accumulations of interest, of which the man himself may not have been aware.

THE SUBMARINE B2 DISASTER.

In connection with the disaster to submarine B2, off Dover, on October 4 last, proceedings have been taken in the King's Bench by Mrs. Bessie Elsie Miller, wife of Mr. W. C. Miller, E.R.A., on behalf of herself and two children, against the owners of the "Amerika," to claim damages, in consequence, as was alleged, of negligent navigation of the "Amerika." As a result of negotiations, the action has been settled, and an order made by the Court for payment by defendants to her and her children of the sum of £1,000—£700 to the widow, and £150 to the public trustee, on behalf of each of the

IN SELF DEFENCE.

At the Dover Police Court on Saturday, before Capt. R. B. Cay and Messrs. G. C. Rubie and J. W. Bussey,

John Taylor, 62, of no fixed abode, was charged with being drunk and disorderly in London Road.

P.C. Leeming said that he was on duty the previous night, at 11.5, and he saw the prisoner in London Road. He commenced fighting. Witness saw that he was very drunk, and he separated the two men, and advised the prisoner to go away, but he would not do so, and being unable to get rid of him, witness took him into custody.

Prisoner: I had a glass of beer in a public-house, with no food all day. When I met the other man, a young man about 19 or 20 years old, he struck me, and dragged me outside, and struck me again, and I struck him. He was with another man. When I struck him, I did so in self-defence.

Chief Inspector Lockwood said the prisoner came into the station earlier in the evening for a casual's ticket.

The Chairman: Will you clear out?—Yes. Where will you go to?—I want to go round towards Brighton.

The police were instructed to see him out of the town.

A DEBTOR'S OPTIMISM.

At a sitting of the East Kent Bankruptcy Court at Canterbury on Saturday, Richard Dryland, of Smeeth, appeared for his public examination. The liabilities were £630 4s. 2d., and there was an estimated surplus of £256 16s. 10d.

Debtor stated that he purchased the business of a brick and tile manufacturer at Brabourne in 1905 for the sum of £360. He raised this money by creating a charge on Chapel Farm and certain pasture land which was willed to him by the former owner. In the same year he became licensee of the Woolpack Inn, Brabourne, and also acquired a fly-driver's business. This latter venture was not a success, and he estimated he lost a sum of from £150 to £200 when he sold it in 1908. He considered the brick and tile business was successful up to two years ago, but since that time the price of labour had increased. He had been handicapped for want of capital, and had had recourse to money lenders.

In reply to the Official Receiver, debtor stoutly maintained that the business would yield a surplus over liabilities of £256. He estimated the growing crops and tenant right

Devon Chronicle, 1913

only a sentence to the fact that John Haigh had been found guilty of fraud in Guildford, Surrey, but the Surrey press devoted columns in several issues to the case. National newspapers generally do not report the vast number of petty crimes with which magistrates' courts and quarter sessions deal. Assize and Crown Court cases from across the country will probably appear in the nationals.

STAND ALONE ARTICLES

Local newspapers, usually published weekly (though not always – the *Sussex Daily News* and the Yorkshire *Telegraph and Argus* are both dailies), will naturally report local crime, much of it being of a petty nature. They do this in a number of ways. First, there can be the stand alone article. These tend to be of what are deemed unusual or serious crimes which merit their own headline. They often go into some detail. They will be of use to both those whose ancestors were accused of criminal activity and those who were victims of crime.

In September 1924 *The West Middlesex Gazette* initially had a short report about a man being arrested and remanded for trial:

ALLEGED CYCLE THEFT
At the Uxbridge Police Court on Tuesday, before Mr H.A. Button, John Reginald Christie, of Southall, was charged with stealing a cycle from the Hillingdon Boys' School on Sept. 11th.
Detective Thrussell said that at 6.30 the previous evening he saw the prisoner lying on the ground in Southall Park. Witness asked him his name and he replied 'Wilson'. He told him that he answered the description of a man who was seen loitering in the vicinity of Hillingdon Boys' school on the afternoon of Sept. 11th, when a bicycle was stolen from the school yard. He replied that he was not there, but did sell a bicycle for a friend of his who lived in Uxbridge, but whose address he did not know. When charged, he persisted in his statement that he never stole it.
Prisoner was remanded until Monday.

Uxbridge Magistrates' Court. Ken Pearce's collection

Incidentally, as already noted, 'police court' is a common term used in the press and an erroneous one. It actually means a magistrates' petty sessions court – the police do not operate courts.

Readers of the newspaper had to wait another week for the finale of this story and this time they were given almost an entire column of newsprint, which also gave much of the prisoner's history, including previous offences.

CYCLE THEFT
FORMER AIRMAN ARRESTED IN SOUTHALL PARK
A REMARKABLE DEFENCE

Previously convicted of stealing postal orders at Halifax for which he was sent to prison for three months, John Reginald Christie (26), a driver of no fixed abode, was said by the Police at Uxbridge Sessions on Monday to have forced an entry into his parents' house at Halifax. His father declined to take proceedings against him.

He was now charged with stealing a bicycle from the Hillingdon Boys' School on September 11th. Detective Thrussell said he saw the prisoner lying on the grass in Southall Park. Witness asked him his name and he replied 'Wilson'. He told him he answered the description of a man who was seen loitering in the vicinity of the Hillingdon Boys' school on the afternoon of September 11th when a bicycle was stolen from the school yard. He replied that he was not there, but did sell a bicycle for a friend of his who lived at Uxbridge, but whose address he did not know. When charged he persisted in his statement that he never stole it.

James Collins, of the Bungalow, Dawley Lodge, a gardener, identified the bicycle which he said, he bought for his son.

SCHOOLBOY'S CYCLE

The boy who said he was twelve years old, told the magistrate that he cycled to school at 1.30 pm and left the machine outside the school building and in view of the road. At three o'clock it was missing.

Ernest Henry Elliott, of High-Street, Southall, a furniture dealer carrying on business at Hayes, said that the prisoner came to him to buy it as he was selling it for a friend of his. Witness said he would try and sell it for him, and put the bicycle in the front of his store and marked it for sale at 35s. Accused called the following day to see if it was sold. He said he wanted to get to work at Uxbridge and could not do so until he had got some money and witness gave him 1s 6d for his fare. He returned later saying he had lost his work through being late. Witness gave him 3s 6d more and told him not to worry him again until the bicycle was sold. A few days later, Saturday September 13th, after witness had sold the bicycle for 35s, the accused called and made an excuse for not bringing his friend to receive the money. As his suspicions were aroused, he informed the police.

Prisoner elected to be dealt with summarily and pleaded

not guilty. He said that when he was discharged from the Royal Air Force in August he became friendly with a man who said he wanted to sell a bicycle. It was not until a week later that that the man brought the machine to him and he rode it to Hayes not knowing it had been stolen. He left it with the dealer and the only money he had had was the 1s 6d to defray expenses. Accused said the man was financially embarrassed and so he helped him with what credit he had from the Air Force. When the dealer asked for his friend to go for the money for the bicycle he waited for him but he failed to turn up and 'so' he added, 'I have to stand here and bear the whole brunt of the charge'.

The Chairman: 'You have not told us the name and address of your friend'.

PREVIOUS CONVICTION
Accused: Jack Smith. I never did know his address, but I gave the police a description of him. My friendship with him started on August 15th, when I was discharged from the Air Force with a good character.

Detective Thrussell said they could find no trace of a man of the description given. The Air Force character which dated from last December to August was 'very good'. His previous history showed him to be a native of Halifax. He went into the Army when he was eighteen years of age and upon his discharge through wounds and gas poisoning he was employed by the postal authorities. He was before the Halifax magistrates on three charges of stealing postal orders and he was sentenced to three months on each charge to run concurrently. On January 15th 1923 he was again before the Halifax magistrates and was placed on probation for falsely obtaining food and lodgings. He had forced an entry into his parents' house but his father declined to take proceedings against him and last year he went to Manchester where it appeared he had been employed as a painter. He joined the

Air Force in December. His parents were very respectable people and had given him every chance.

The Chairman told the accused that the magistrates did not believe his story and would convict.

THEFTS FROM CINEMA

Accused was now further charged with stealing from the Empire Cinema, Uxbridge, £5 9s in coppers, a quantity of cigarettes, a packet of chocolates, and a glass cutter, together the value of £5 18s 2d.

Elizabeth Miller of 29 Vine Street, Uxbridge, a cleaner and attendant at the Cinema, said she knew the accused who was an operator at the Cinema about the end of last year. On Sunday, August 24th, the operator named Needham, and his assistant, were at the theatre when the accused came in and began working on the dynamo. Needham appeared to know nothing about the accused, but helped him to do the work. She locked up the place in the evening: the following morning she found the front doors in Vine-Street unbolted.

John Polley, the manager, said the accused was the operator at the cinema from December 20th to February 20th. Witness reached the hall at about 3 o'clock on Monday afternoon, August 25th, and upon opening his office door he found a chair obstructing it. Looking round he saw a pipe and an R.A.F. glove lying on the desk. The cash which had been placed in the drawer ready for the bank on Monday, was missing, as was also a quantity of cigarettes, a packet of chocolate, five business cards of travellers who called on him and a glass cutter. The cards and the glass cutter now produced he identified as his property.

Detective Thrussell said that when he arrested the prisoner he took possession of the glass cutter and the five business cards.

DETECTIVE COMMENDED

Accused pleaded not guilty and said he went and repaired the generator at Needham's request, and they walked away from the cinema together.

Mr Polley said that he did not authorise the accused to repair the generator.

The Bench found him guilty.

Prisoner said he joined the R.A.F. with the idea of getting out of the country to reform, but owing to the reaction of gas poisoning due to the war he was discharged. He asked to be dealt with as leniently as possible and promised to do his best in the future.

He was sent to prison for three months hard labour for stealing the bicycle and a further six months hard labour for stealing the money etc. from the Cinema.

The Bench highly commended Detective Thrussell on showing considerable acumen in the bicycle case.

Now, this is an extremely detailed account of what was essentially petty theft. It provides more detail than many murder cases would elicit in modern newspapers. This is in part due to the smaller text in older newspapers and in part due to the higher level of crime in more recent years. There is much about the prisoner's past history, both his previous crimes being mentioned and his previous careers in the postal service, the cinema and in the RAF; both the first and the last employers are now venues for additional research as copious staff records are kept for both services. The Halifax press should also be examined for further details about his previous offences and these are gone into in some depth, too. Incidentally, books about this criminal, who went on to commit far more serious offences, and a film about him, always cite his second Halifax offence as being one involving violence; both this report and that in the Halifax newspaper give the lie to these oft repeated statements.

There are limitations to this piece of newspaper reporting, as is the case with reports of most crimes in the press. They do not state in which prison/s he served his time in and how long he spent there. Despite being given a nine-month sentence, prisoners who behave well in prison are given remission, i.e. time off for good behaviour, so that a model prisoner given a nine-month sentence would be at liberty before that time. The researcher then needs to check the admission registers for prisons; possibly several will need to be checked to find the correct one as it will not necessarily be the one nearest to the court, but at least the researcher now knows the date of admission which will almost always be the same date as the day of the court's verdict. For prison records, see Chapter 3. Other details of the report, if possible, should be checked, too. In this instance, though the accused's aged is given as 26, it was actually 25.

'POLICE COURT' HEARINGS

The local press will also report the activities of the local magistrates' courts or petty sessions. Apart from those cases deemed interesting enough in their own merit, there can be summaries of other cases, often quite minor, under the aforementioned general heading. This will be a round-up of a week's worth of court hearings. One newspaper even termed this column 'Your Neighbour in Court'.

Not all cases heard will be reported here. Only a sample of offences (by no means all) which came before the court are noted. These appear in each edition as a routine feature, as the newspaper sends a reporter to the court hearings to make notes of what happened there (the young Charles Dickens briefly worked in this capacity in the early 1830s). These normally list date of hearing, defendant (and address) and give synopses of the offence, what was said and the verdict, with punishment allotted, if any. They tend to be of a more petty and routine nature than those mentioned above. They include offences such as begging, use of improper language, drunk and disorderly, offences towards animals and domestic violence, drug and motor offences.

The Middlesex County Times in November 1876 gave summary reports of a number of offences as follows:

THE MIDDLESEX

BRENTFORD.

PETTY SESSIONS, Saturday, September 4.

Before J. R. Hogarth, Esq. (in the chair), F. Ashton, Esq., and General Tremenheere.

Mary Turner was summoned f r using abusive and indecent language in the Half Acre, Old Brentford, on the 9th August.

PC 277 T proved the offence, which defendant denied, but the Bench, nevertheless, fined her 10s, or seven days' imprisonment.

TO LAUNDRYMEN.

Henry Bradbury, laundryman, of Twickenham, appeared in answer to an adjourned summons charging him with unlawfully detaining certain articles of wearing apparel belonging to Mr. William Hawthorn.

The case was opened on the previous Saturday, but inasmuch as complainant was not then in a position to prove the delivery of the articles into the possession of defendant, the case was adjourned.

Mr. Briggs now appeared for comp'ainant and Mr. Mitton for defendant.

Several witnesses, including Mrs. Hawthorn and servants, were called and proved that the articles in question were delivered to defendant to be washed and that they had never been returned. It was admitted by complainant that he was indebted to the defendant in the sum of £2 17s for three weeks' washing, but that this amount he had offered to pay immediately the missing articles were surrendered.

The order of the court was that the things be given up or their equivalent in money, amounting to £4 8s 6d less £2 17s 6d for the washing.

THE FACTORY ACT.

John Felloes, of East Acton, was charged with unlawfully employing a lad under the age of 16 years.

Mr. Henderson, sub-inspecter of factories for the district, proved the case, and defendant was fined 20s, or 14 days.

James Clarke, of Hounslow, and *John Dean*, of Kew Bridge, were similarly charged under the same statute.

The first named was fined 20s, or 14 days', and the last-named, who had employed a little girl under twelve in a brickfield, was fined 40s, or a month's imprisonment.

DEFECTIVE WEIGHTS AND MEASURES.

William Sketchley, of the King's Head, Twickenham, was summoned by Mr. J. Gregg, inspector of weights and measures, for having a number of defective measures in his possession on the 25th August.

Mr. J. Haynes defended, and pointed out that defendant had not long been in the house. The measures were very old ones, and being covered with dents they did not hold the imperial quantity.

Fined 20s.

James Mortlock, of Brentford, was summoned for having five unjust weights and a pair of scales in his possession.

Mr. Stephen Woodbridge defended, and stated that Mr. Mortlock had been in business for a great number of years during which time there had never before been any discrepancy in his scales and weights. The fact was defendant contracted with a tradesman to attend to his weights, and the reason they were defective at the present time was that they had not been attended to for a little longer time.

The Bench thought there was no intention to defraud on the part of the defendant, and fined him 20s for the weights and 10s for the scales.

William Pocock and *William Goode* were each fined 20s for similar offences.

JUVENILE OFFENDERS.

Four lads, named respectively *Henry Waters*, *William Renton*, *Joseph Palmer*, and *Henry Millet*, were fined 2s 6d each for stealing fruit from a garden at Hanwell belonging to Messrs. Tusden and Rooke, brewers, of Notting-hill.

POLICE COURT.

MONDAY.

Before J. R. Hogarth, Esq., (in the chair), and F. Ashton, Esq.

John Holt was charged with being drunk and disorderly at Ealing, on Sunday evening.

PC 53 X said he saw prisoner, he being drunk, and annoying the passengers by pushing them oft the footpath.

This being prisoner's first offence he was fined 10s or seven days.

Albert Robinson, a lad, was charged with being found on the enclosed premises of Mr. Thomas Mitton, at Lampton, in the parish of Heston.

PC 190 T said last Saturday night he was on duty in Lampton. About eight o'clock he saw prisoner clambering over the wall out of the garden. He asked the lad what he was doing but he made no reply. Witness then said he should take prisoner to Mr. Mitton.

Prosecutor stated that a few days prior to the offence he was standing in his stable-yard when he was struck on the side of the head with a missile. Being sworn, prosecutor said he saw prisoner on his premises on the night in question; he had seen the lad there numbers of times before.

it was lost. On the near side of the cart one of the wooden wings that cover the wheel was broken, through an accident, and I had it mended, and on the near side wheel one of the spokes was bent by the same accident. I saw the cart yesterday at the police-station, Hampstead. It is the same body as when it was lost, but some alterations have been made to it—the iron portion has been replaced with brass—and I can identify the cart as the one I sold to my master.

Cross examined—The cart I saw on the 7th ult. had three springs, one on each side and one under the body. Prisoner said he lent Mr. Kingswell the cart.

PC Durham, 111 T, said about five o'clock on Monday afternoon I went to 33, Bayswater-street, Chelsea, where I saw the prisoner, and said I had come to see him about a cart which was in the possession of a man named Kingswell. He replied "Yes, the cart is mine. I bought it at Smithfield, and gave £5 for it, and afterwards paid £4 8s 0d to have it done up." I asked the prisoner then to go with me to Hampstead, where we saw Inspector Jones, and he repeated the same statement to him. I then brought him to Chelsea station, where he was detained. A man named Charles Kingswell was charged at Hampstead for the unlawful possession of the cart, and he is now under remand. The receipt for £5 15s from a Mr. Simpson for a cart was handed to me by the prisoner's wife the same evening.

Henry Jones, inspector of the T division, gave corroborative evidence as to what took place at Hampstead, and asked for a remand.

Mr. Mitton urged that the evidence was insufficient, the cart not being produced; but

The Chairman thought it conclusive, and remanded the case, refusing to take bail.

BRENTFORD LOCAL BOARD.

The usual monthly meeting of this Board was held at the Town Hall, on Tuesday. There were present—Mr. C. J. Cross (in the chair), Messrs. Clarke, Layton, Besly, Jupp, W. Barnes, Carpenter, Figg, H. and S. Barnes; Mr. F. Davies (medical officer), Mr. S. Woodbridge (clerk), and Mr. Gatwood (surveyor).

The minutes of the last meeting were read and confirmed.

THE FINANCE COMMITTEE

Reported that they had examined the Surveyor's accounts for the past three weeks showing a balance of £2 15s 1d. It was recommended that the sum of £15 be drawn to meet the expenses of the current fortnight. The expenses of the Fire Brigade at the late fire at Mr. Phillips', of Hounslow, were announced as £3 1s. The report further stated that the audit by the District Auditor (G. Gibson, Esq.) had passed off without any surcharges or alterations being made in the accounts.

On the motion of Messrs. Clarke and Jupp, the report was adopted.

TREASURER'S REPORT.

It was reported that the Treasurer had a balance in hand amounting to £505 2s 7d.

BOSTON PARK ROAD.

Mr. JUPP called attention to an offensive smell arising from the rubbish that was being deposited under the surface gravel in the Boston Park-road.

Mr. DAVIES (the medical officer) stated that he had, by request, visited the locality referred to and the odour from the refuse reminded him of that proceeding from a dust heap; it was not injurious to health. He suggested the advisability of the road being rolled as in its present state he pitied the poor oxen that had to travel over it.

Mr. JUPP said the effluvium was very disagreeable, and there was a fear amongst the inhabitants that a fever would be propagated thereby. It was resolved to allow the contractor to proceed with the work and that the Surveyor suggest to him the necessity for the road being rolled on completion.

THE AUDIT.

The following is an extract from a letter addressed to the Clerk by G. Gibson, Esq., (District Auditor):—"I have to report to you for the information of the Local Board of Health for the District of Brentford that on the 2nd September I concluded the audit of the Board's accounts for the year ended Lady Day, 1875. I found the accounts for the above period had been well kept, and the payments credited to the Treasurer, supported by the requisite vouchers, and my certificate to this effect will be found entered on the Board's ledger."

This was considered very satisfactory, and the necessary orders were given to the Clerk to publish the accounts in the usual way.

A COMPLAINT.

The resident engineer at the Waterworks, Kew-bridge wrote to the Inspector of Nuisances—who reported on the matter—complaining of the offensive smell proceeding from two barges stationed in the river and containing a quantity of refuse to be used in the making up of Boston Park-road, Brentford.

The CLERK observed that after what the medical officer had stated he did not think it necessary to take any action in the matter.

TENDERS FOR GRANITE.

In answer to advertisement for the supply of 500

thern, £24 3s 6½d; and Southern, £30 1s 5d. Total, £105 2s. 8½d.

TREASURER'S BALANCE.

The balance in the hands of the Treasurer was reported to be £2,384 2s 4d; including £17 2s paid in by Mr. Brown; £41 10s by Greenford; and £164 by Acton.

It was ordered that the several amounts be posted to the credit of the proper accounts and debit of the treasurers.

CHEQUES.

Cheques not presented—£25 0s. 0d.

The following cheques were issued on the recommendation of the Finance Committee to the relieving officers:—Eastern district, £30, Southern £20, Western £15 Northern, £15.

Per bill book—£42 16s 11d.

Orders were accordingly drawn on the Treasurers for the accounts to be posted to the credit of the Treasurer, and debit of the accounts chargeable therewith.

QUESTION OF POWER.

An unusual case came before the Board, in which the powers of the authorities of National Schools to refuse to admit a child were discussed. A widow named Wells, in receipt of relief, was examined as to the reason she had not sent her child, eight years old, to school, as the orders of the Local Government Board require the attendance at school of the children of pauper parents.

The woman replied that her son was a very bad boy and the authorities of the National School, Hounslow, would not take him in the school.

The Board questioned the competency of the authorities to refuse admission to a child, seeing that the school was supported by the parish; and in the end the clerk was instructed to write to the Rev. Mr. East for further information.

INSPECTION OF LUNATICS.

Dr. Davies wrote forwarding a report concerning the lunatics at the Hanwell and Colney Hatch Asylums, which was of a satisfactory character.

THE SANITARY AUTHORITY

then held their usual fortnighly meeting.

The CLERK reported that he had placed himself in communication with the Local Government Board on the subject of the formation of the districts of Heston and Isleworth as a separate Sanitary Authority, and in reply he had received the following letter:—

"Local Government Board, Whitehall, S W.,
"7th September, 1875.

"SIR,—I am directed by the Local Government Board to advert to the Provisional Order, dated the 5th June last, constituting the Heston and Isleworth Urban Sanitary District, and to state that it has now been confirmed by Parliament.

"I am directed to point out that under Article II of the Order in question the first election of the members of the Local Board in this district is to be conducted in the manner prescribed by law where a Local Board is elected in a place with a known and a defined boundary in which there is no churchwarden or overseer. It is therefore necessary that the returning officer, who is to conduct the election, should be appointed by the Board, and they are desirous of being furnished with the names of two or three suitable persons who would be willing to undertake the duties of the office, if appointed, and who do not intend to become candidates for election as members of the Local Board, or clerk to the Local Board when elected. The Board direct me to add that they would be glad to receive the names of such persons as early as practicable in order that the necessary appointment may shortly be made and that the requisite arrangements for holding the election may be effected in time to allow of the notices of the election being issued as soon after the 29th as possible.—I am, sir, your obedient servant,
"H. FLEMING,
"Secretary."

In accordance with the request contained in the letter the Board mentioned the name of Mr. Ruston.

This concluded the business.

CRICKET.—GUARDIANS v. OFFICERS.

A peculiarly interesting game of cricket was played in the recreation meadow, facing the workhouse at Isleworth, on Wednesday, between eleven members of the Board of Guardians and an equal number of the officers of the union. The idea of this match originated with Mr. Hardy, of Chiswick, and it was at once fallen in with by his brother Guardians, and the arrangements for the contest on the part of the Guardians were entrusted to Mr. Hardy, and Mr. R. W. Pittard on the part of the officers. This is the first match of the kind that has taken place in connection with this union, but we believe it is intended to make it an annual event and as such will serve to mani-

Middlesex County Times, 1875

CRUELTY TO A PONY

Mrs McCormack, a Hammersmith laundress, was summoned for allowing a pony to be worked while in an unfit state.

Mr Mitton prosecuted, on behalf of the Society for the Prevention of Cruelty to Animals.

The woman pleaded for leniency, stating that she had experienced heavy losses during the last twelve months, being 'let in' with two horses.

The magistrates, having fined her 10s and costs, Mr Mitton applied for his fee, and after some consideration, was allowed the 10s.

ASLEEP

Wm. Mitchell of Iver, was summoned for riding asleep while in charge of two horses at Ealing, and was fined 10s.

CLOSING OF WELLS

Mrs Hinge, who did not appear, was summoned by the owner of Rose Cottage, Factory Yard, Hanwell, to shew cause why a well of water should not be closed, the same being polluted and injurious to health.

Dr R.G. Ruston, medical officer of health the Hanwell Rural Sanitary Authority, said he examined a sample of water on the 30th October, and found a large quantity of organic matter suspended in it, this rendering it quite unfit for drinking purposes. He should say that it was highly dangerous.

Mr Hailey, the inspector, deposed to procuring the sample, and added that Mrs Hinge was having water laid on before, but the fault laid with the tradesman who had been engaged to do the work.

The magistrates made an order for the well to be at once closed permanently.

Mr John Marks was summoned in respect of three wells of polluted water at Hanwell.

The case was called on at the previous Sessions, but was

adjourned because it was stated the wells were being closed.

Mr Hailey now said the work was in progress, but only one had been closed at present.

The magistrates ordered all three to be closed.

THE TRADE IN FIREWORKS

Charles Evan Goddard, fancy dealer, of New Brentford, was summoned for keeping fireworks on his premises in an unlawful manner, and also for selling fireworks to a boy apparently under the age of 13.

Mr Haynes, prosecuted on behalf of Mr Gregg, Inspector for the district, and Mr G.W. Lay defended.

Both cases were substantiated, and the Bench inflicted a fine of 20s, or 14 days imprisonment in each case.

Several other summonses of a similar character were heard, and convictions entered in all of them.

UNJUST WEIGHTS

Frederick Nash, marine store dealer of Brentford, was summoned by Mr Gregg, Inspector of weights and measures, for having four deficient weights in his possession, and also an unjust balance.

Defendant pointed out that as he bought with the weights instead of selling the deficiency was against himself.

The deficiency in the balance was very slight, and the magistrates only imposed a fine of 10s for the two offences, the Chairman remarking that they did not consider defendant had any intention of defrauding his customers at all.

This is how most fairly minor crime is reported; recent newspapers tend to give name, age and address of defendant, charge and sentence if any. The importance of newspapers is that for the vast majority of trials there is no transcript of what was actually said. The reporting is the reporter's paraphrase but it is the only record of that trial (or inquest) apart from the formal details as found in court registers and assize papers (or coroners' papers). It is to be hoped that the journalist correctly reported details, though the facts stated may or may not be truthful, as in the case of the *Acton Gazette*'s reporting of the inquest of Montague John Druitt in January 1889, for which, see below.

INQUESTS

The majority of coroners' reports do not survive; there is no legal obligation for more than a small handful to exist. Even where they do survive, they are usually closed for seventy-five years. Newspapers do report inquests – not only accidental deaths but those of manslaughter, murder and suicide (the latter being a crime until 1961) – and so are often the only source of accessing any information about an inquest.

The following is a report of an inquest taken from the *Acton Gazette* of 5 January 1889:

> FOUND DROWNED-Shortly after mid-day on Monday, a waterman named Winslade, of Chiswick, found the body of a man, well dressed, floating on the Thames off Thorneycroft's. He at once informed a constable, and without delay the body was conveyed on the ambulance to the mortuary. On Wednesday afternoon, Dr Diplock, coroner, held the inquest at the Lamb Tap, where the following evidence was adduced – William H. Druitt said he lived at Bournemouth, and that he was a solicitor. The deceased was his brother, who was 31 last birthday. He was a barrister-at-law, and an assistant master in a school at Blackheath, He had stayed with witness at Bournemouth for a night towards the end of October. Witness heard from a friend on the 11th December that deceased had not been heard of at his chambers for more than a week. Witness then went to London to make inquiries, and at Blackheath he found that deceased had got into serious trouble at the school, and had been dismissed. That was on the 30th December. Witness had deceased's things searched

Winchester Coroners' Court. Author.

where he resided, and found a paper addressed to him (produced). The Coroner read the letter, which was to this effect, 'Since Friday I felt I was going to be like mother, and the best thing for me was to die'. Witness, continuing, said deceased had never made any attempt on his life before. His mother became insane in July last. He had no other relative. Henry Winslade was the next witness. He said that he lived at No. 4 Shore Street, Paxton road, and that he was a water-man. About one o'clock on Monday he was on the river in a boat, when he saw the body floating. The tide was at half flood, running up. He brought the body ashore and gave information to the police. P.C. George Moulsdon, 216T, said he searched the body, which was fully dressed, excepting a hat and collar. He found four large stones in each pocket in the top coat; £2 10s in gold, 7s in silver, 2d. in bronze, two cheques on the London and Provincial Bank (one for £20 and the other for £16), a first class season pass from Blackheath to London

(South Western Railway), a second half return Hammersmith to Charing Cross (dated 1st December), a silver watch, gold chain with a spade guinea attached. There were no papers or letters of any kind. There were no marks of injury on the body, but it was rather decomposed. A verdict of suicide whilst in an unsound state of mind was returned.

Of course, a report may not be wholly correct; in the above instance, Druitt was not the deceased's only relation and clearly the dating of the dismissal should be 30 November – nor is the deceased named.

Apart from magistrates' court hearings, crime can be reported where initially – if ever – the perpetrator is unknown. This is often the case with thefts, such as burglaries, where a newspaper may report a spate of burglaries in a locality, giving victim, address, property stolen and other particulars. A stabbing might be reported, or another offence where the instigator is not initially known. These might dwell on the victim, rather than the accused, whereas the reporting of court hearings inevitably focus on the accused.

These reports often include biographical information on the accused and their victim, including, perhaps, previous offences. In the case of murder victims there may be an extensive biography of the deceased, especially if they are middle aged or elderly or are in any way prominent locally or nationally. In the case of Vera Page, aged 10, who was assaulted and murdered in Notting Hill in 1931 there was relatively little to say in *The Kensington News*, but when Ernest Key was killed in his shop in Surbiton seven years later, there was an extensive account in *The Surrey Comet* of the life and career of this jeweller, who was a mason and had fingers in many pies. On the other hand, there may be nothing. The Kensington newspapers had nothing to say about the young life of Beryl Evans, murdered locally in 1949. How accurate newspaper accounts of the life of a crime victim is another question, for it is rare for unfavourable comment to be made about someone whose life is cut short and, with friends and family supplying the information, the impression given is that victims of crime are little short of saintly. Cross-referencing newspaper accounts with other sources is recommended.

MAJOR CRIME

Most of the cases that come before magistrates' courts, and which are reported as mentioned above, tend to appear once in a newspaper and then that is that. Only unusually interesting cases will take up more than a paragraph or two in a single issue of a local newspaper. Serious crime will take up several issues in both the local and national press. There can be lengthy reports of trials and the lead-up to them, including investigations, preliminary hearings and so forth. They will be covered by several newspapers. Clearly the newspaper for the place where the crime was committed will cover it, as will the place where it was tried (if different) but so will newspapers where the defendant/victim came from, if different from those already mentioned.

In some cases, crime cases will be reported over a number of issues. This is usually the case with particularly serious and/or contentious cases. If no one is charged at the onset, then a case develops a fascination of its own. This is especially so if a number of clues are found and witnesses come forward. Often these can be unearthed by journalists as well as detectives. They tend to fuel speculation and theories begin to be developed, often on very tenuous grounds, and these are circulated throughout other newspapers.

Once a suspect has been arrested, the motions of the law begin to turn and these hearings are chronicled. Often they are heard first in a magistrates' court and later are heard in an assize court, often over a number of days or weeks. This will occur in murder cases, but also in other cases as well. If there is a lengthy police investigation, this may be chronicled in the press, but a newspaper will often only give a summary of what steps are being taken to pursue the criminal/s.

Murder trials were a favourite from the mid-nineteenth to the mid-twentieth century. National daily, Sunday and weekly newspapers devoted a great deal of space to them, providing synopses of the speeches made by counsel for the Crown prosecuting and the barrister defending the prisoner, examinations and cross-examinations of witnesses by each side, the summing up speeches by both barristers, and then by the judge, verdict and finally the sentence. Reports of these trials would last several days. These were detailed but were not word for word accounts of what was said in court and they might not report on every single witness. Reporters might also describe how the defendant and others appeared. Coverage varied enormously.

The Times newspaper covered a tragic domestic double murder in two short paragraphs. On 5 December 1949 they reported:

ALLEGED MURDER OF A WIFE
Timothy John Evans, 25, motor driver, of no fixed address, was charged at West London on Saturday with the murder of his wife Mrs Beryl Evans, 19, at Rillington Place, Notting Hill, W., on Nov. 8. The bodies of Mrs Evans and of her 14 month old daughter, Geraldine, were found on Friday in the wash-house behind their home. Evans was remanded in custody until December 15.

On 10 March 1950 there was the following:

MURDERER HANGED
Timothy John Evans, 25, lorry driver, of Rillington Place, Notting Hill, W, was executed yesterday at Pentonville, for the murder of Geraldine, his 14 month old daughter on December 2. Evans was sentenced to death at the Central Criminal court on January 13.

Sunday newspapers would often pay for the defence of the accused and in return receive his or her life story as an exclusive, to be published after the trial. The now defunct tabloids the *Sunday Pictorial* and *News of the World* published those of notorious killers

Newspaper photograph of John Christie. The Author

Neville Heath and John Haigh in the late 1940s for example. How accurate their stories were are another question. Often the stories would be highly selective and ghost written by the journalists who interviewed them. In any case, criminals would tend to write in a way that would downplay the enormity of their offences and try and include details of their character and interests that would strike a chord with the actual reader, such as the killer liking children and animals. Sensationalist aspects of the case would be emphasised.

Newspapers can be very ambivalent about victims of crime. Some cast aspersions on the victim's character. When Irene Munro was murdered in 1920 an initial witness to be interviewed was her mother who stressed her daughter's respectability: never going to dances and not having a boyfriend. Yet when the girl's friends and colleagues were interviewed, a different story emerged; one of a girl who went to restaurants and theatres with men who paid for her. It was known she had a French friend and an elderly wealthy man who enjoyed her company. All this, appearing in the *Daily Mail* and the *News of the World*, was beginning to look rather suggestive. The fact that she was not a virgin, though irrelevant to the case, was also noted in the press. Yet a subsequent article in the former newspaper put matters right, 'Possibly frivolous but still innocent, Irene Munro had undoubtedly a large circle of men friends, friends who were unknown to her relatives, but her relationship to them was that of a girl who liked the bright life of cafes and restaurants and nothing more.'

Initial reporting can get things wrong and reporting can often sensationalise findings. In the case of the Bamber family killed in their Essex home in 1985, the newspapers first highlighted that Shelia Bamber had killed her parents and children before turning the gun in herself and there were dramatic comments made about both her (as a drug-addled lunatic) and her mother (as a religious fanatic who was in conflict with her daughter). Admittedly this was not far from what the police were assuming was the truth. It was only a few weeks later that an alternative and more truthful version of events emerged which cast the crimes in a rather different light.

The moral of the story is then not to accept at face value what the newspapers state.

At the other extreme, victims can become almost canonised. A recent Ealing murder victim who was also a drug dealer had his death reported in a most sympathetic light. Friends and family rushed to give tributes that he had many virtues and values, though whether those affected by the products of his trade would have been equally fulsome is another matter.

Until the twentieth century newspapers were rarely illustrated, but by the early twentieth century they would include photographs of the victim/s, defendant, lawyers, police officers, witnesses, crime scenes, pathologists, relatives of the deceased, the defendant and others involved. These would often be taken when these people were going to or from the court – pictures cannot be taken in court or in prisons or police stations, of course. There might be maps and plans, too. This did not always happen, however.

One exception to this general rule about pictures is *The Illustrated Police News*, founded in 1864 and which ran until 1938. Contrary to the title, it had nothing to do with the police force, but was a weekly tabloid aimed at the newly literate masses of Victorian Britain and those seeking sensationalist news. It reported war, disasters, human interest stories, sport and crime. What was more, in contrast to the majority of newspapers, it was profusely illustrated with line drawings – not photographs – often based on the imaginations of the journalists or those employed by the newspaper as artists. They would draw pictures of the majority of the key characters in crime cases as well as crime scenes or buildings associated with it. In some cases these are the only pictures which appeared in the press of these people. *The Illustrated London News*, founded in 1852, was another newspaper, covering far more than just London, that was also good for pictures of nineteenth-century crime.

Another newspaper, if that is the right word for it, is the weekly *The Police Gazette*, which began existence in 1772 as *Hue and Cry*, became *Hue and Cry and Police Gazette* in 1797, was renamed *Police Gazette; or Hue and Cry* in 1828 and adopted its present name in

1839. It was initially free of charge and was issued by the Bow Street Magistrates' Court in London but eventually began to be issued to all police stations in the country. It listed people that the law was interested in: missing persons, escaped convicts, those suspected of crime, army deserters and so on. It would provide detailed descriptions of them. Editions for the years 1812–1902 and from 1921–7 can be found on the Ancestry website, where they can be searched by name. Access to later twentieth-century copies is often restricted as those mentioned therein may still be alive and application will need to be made to Scotland Yard to gain permission for limited access for a specific reason (in my experience for cases in the 1940s, I have had no problem here).

To give a brief example of the type of material to be found, the following paragraph comes from *The Police Gazette* for 1927:

N. Division
For embezzlement – Mary Flowers, b.1867, 5 ft, short build, h[air].dk (turning grey), e[yes]. brown, North Country accent; dress, long black coat, blue skirt, black hat (trimmed black feather). Was employed as deputy at a lodging house, collected money from lodgers, and absconded. Warrant issued.

This is particularly valuable as it may be the only physical description of the person in question.

SOURCES

There are many places where old newspapers can be found. A great deal of research can now take place from the comfort of your own home if you are prepared to pay for it. Or you can visit an institution where such online facilities are available for free for members.

The online sources have multiplied in recent years and continue to grow. The main site is www.britishnewspaperarchive.co.uk for it includes many newspapers published in Britain and elsewhere for many years, from the late seventeenth century to the late twentieth century, though its coverage of the past half century is patchy. It is a

British Library. Author

ten-year project to put 40 million pages of newspapers online. It can also be found as part of the FindmyPast and Genes Reunited sites. Its index can be searched by keyword free of charge, and can be narrowed down by date, but once articles with that keyword are located a reader must either pay the subscription fee demanded or visit an institution where access is provided free of charge, such as the British Library. Ancestry has only a very few newspapers and magazines on its site.

There are other online newspapers such as *The Times*, available at many public libraries, and the *Manchester Guardian* (which was an important newspaper for Manchester news up to the mid-nineteenth century as well as the only left-wing broadsheet in the later twentieth century) which can be accessed by Manchester Local Studies Library's website for free. Or copies of it and the *Observer* from 1791 to 2003 can be accessed at http://pqasb.pqarchives.com/ guardian. The *Daily Mirror* and *Daily Mail* are also available online for a fee. The *Daily Mirror* and other newspapers can be accessed on www.ukpressonline.co.uk. Welsh newspapers from 1844 to 1910 can be seen online at http://welshnewspapers.llgc.org.uk. Google news archives on http://news.google.com/newspapers includes three Glaswegian newspapers for the nineteenth and twentieth centuries. The *Irish Times* can be seen on www.irishtimes.com/premium/loginpage. *The Scotsman* from 1817 to 1950 can be viewed at http://archives.scotsman.com. A subscription fee is payable to view the articles but the indexes can be searched for free. Some institutions subscribe to these but it is usual to have to visit them to do so.

Searching by keyword is a marvellous way of finding individuals who would never be found otherwise; minor offences can be located thus, as can the innocuous activities of victims. So can articles which are relevant but which were reported weeks, months or years after the event that a conventional search would never bring up. Some more general family history websites contain some newspapers online, though sometimes they are read-only rather than searchable by keyword. The effectiveness of keyword searches is also dependent on how clear the original text of the newspaper is as words may not be readable if one or more letters are indistinct, as some are.

However, the bulk of newspapers are not yet available online. The majority of newspapers can be seen at the British Library's Newspaper Room (now housed at the main Library at St Pancras, London, not at Colindale). These are usually on microfilm (see http://catalogue.bl.uk and search under Newspaper Library for the titles and dates available there for order) but occasionally, and especially for local newspapers, as hard copy there. These mostly have to be ordered in advance, but for some, especially those on microfilm, the waiting time is only seventy minutes; most of the hard copy is at the out store at Boston Spa in Yorkshire and forty-eight hours' notice is needed, assuming it is in a fit condition to be seen. Microfilmed newspapers can be copied easily, however, and pages can be sent to the researchers' email address, thus saving time and money in making copies.

Local studies/history libraries will hold the local press for their districts, again usually on microfilm. These may be indexed, but clearly not on the same level as the online versions and indexers rarely index every crime – too many of them – but major offences may well be indexed and it may be possible to trace the developments in such cases from the actual crime itself to the court case and beyond.

A major difficulty with using the newspapers as a source is that they can often be factually unreliable. This is in part due to the speed with which they are written in order to meet a tight deadline, which is especially the case with daily newspapers where the story has to appear by next morning. Unlike historians, the journalist rarely has the luxury of being able to cross-check facts and rewrite if need be. There is also a limited amount of space for a story as it has to compete with other stores in that edition of the newspaper.

Journalists tend to receive their information from three main sources; from official press conferences with police representatives in which a prepared statement is read out and then questions can be asked. They also may obtain information from police officers informally – traditionally this was by visiting the pubs that officers drank in. They may also speak to witnesses and other members of the public with relevant information, with crime reporters acting as amateur sleuths much to the annoyance of the police. In the case of trials they will often be present to take notes but not photographs from the part of the courtroom reserved for them. But they will not be privy to all the information that the police have, such as forensic evidence and information from witnesses as well as letters and other communications. The lack of official reports often leads journalists to speculate with their own theories, interview locals themselves or/and criticise the police, especially if an arrest is not made soon after the crime.

The question is, if a date of an event is known, which newspapers should be checked, other than those available online. National newspapers will cover major crimes, of course. Local newspapers are useful for the lesser crimes (unless such are carried out by a well-known personage and then that is national news). Clearly the newspaper which covers the location where the crime took must be consulted. Secondly, if the miscreant lived elsewhere, the local newspaper covering his/her home town might also cover them. When Montague John Druitt committed suicide in the Thames in 1888 his death was recorded in the district where he died (*Acton Gazette*) and also where he lived (Blackheath in Kent, so this was recorded in *The Kentish Mercury*). It does not seem to have been deemed of national significance, however.

Criminals and their activities tend to receive far more column space than their victims. Virtually nothing was reported about Beryl Evans following her murder, except for a Kensington newspaper to mention which school in the district she had attended and another which gave a brief adulatory statement from an old school friend.

Newspapers are a vital source for family historians investigating ancestors who have been involved in crime. The amount of information varies considerably. If a crime is brought to trial there will be far more than if it is not, though not necessarily – for the Whitechapel murders of 1888 dominated the press for weeks in that 'Autumn of Terror'. Newspapers can help flesh out what would otherwise be bare bones of court records. As with all research, they need to be cross-referenced with other sources. Local newspapers are usually the key source, but the national press may have also covered it if it was of sufficient interest. If a case is covered by several newspapers, there will be much repetition therein (looking at an event in ten different newspapers will not give ten times the information found in one), but there may be additional information. As ever, it is a matter of knowing when to stop and only the individual researcher can decide that for themselves.

Chapter 6

BOOKS

Books about crime are common. They serve to satisfy the demands of a reading public that has grown throughout the centuries. They can be written for entertainment, information, to serve a moral or political point or a number of these. Unlike other sources they bring together a narrative of the events in question in one place. Shortly after a major or sensational crime, it is common for a book or booklet to be produced to cash in on the notoriety, often written by someone with direct knowledge of the case. There are two main sources we shall examine here: primary sources, written at the time of the events or shortly afterwards, often by those actually involved in them, and those written long after the event by historians and others. Both have their weaknesses and strengths and both should deal with criminals and their victims.

PRIMARY SOURCES: TRIALS

Before the advent of newspapers in the seventeenth century, information about famous trials was cobbled together by printers and sold in pamphlet form. These flesh out what exists in the assize records and give a greater insight into the world in which these crimes took place. A pamphlet, *The examination and confession of certain wytches at Chemsforde in the Countie of Essex before the Quenes majesties Judges, the XXVI daye of July Anno 1566*, printed in the same year, described a trial at the Chelmsford Assizes. Elizabeth Francis was alleged to have bewitched a child causing it to become 'decrepit' and so was sentenced to a year in gaol. Apparently Elizabeth, who had been responsible for many other forms of witchcraft, was motivated to such acts because a wealthy man had refused to marry her, 'Wherefore she willed Satan to touch his body which he forthwith did whereof he died'. Agnes Waterhouse was accused of similar crimes in the same pamphlet; chiefly because of her disputes with her neighbours she and her familiar killed three hogs of one, drowned another's three geese and bewitched the curds of yet another.

There have been other accounts of trials which have been published. The Edinburgh publisher, Henry Hodges, at the beginning of the twentieth century, employed editors to work on particularly notorious trials dating from the sixteenth century onwards. This series was titled *Notable British Trials*. These would include a transcript of the trial, with the complete speeches of judge, counsels for prosecution and defence, witnesses and others. There would be an introduction to the case and numerous appendices with additional comment to help illuminate the case and those involved in it. Maps, plans and photographs would also be included. The series came to an end in the 1950s with the final volume covering Christie and Evans. Most of the trials it dealt with were murders, but there were some treason trials.

Although of huge interest, especially if they dealt with a case from 1907 onwards in which the accused could speak in their own defence, so their words can be read, the role of victims tends to be downplayed. For instance, in the volume dealing with the inconclusive trial of John Donald Merrett in Edinburgh in 1927 on the charges of murdering his mother and forging her cheques, not very much is said about his mother in the introduction. We do, though, learn what some of her friends and relatives had to say about her (mostly very favourable, of course) and so that is of use.

To take an example of the text of a trial, here is the deadly cross-examination of Timothy Evans, on trial for the murder of his daughter in 1950, by Christmas Humphreys KC:

Humphreys asked:
'And you were asking for that charge of murder to be made against you in order to protect a man who you now say is the murderer, is that right?'
'Yes'

'Why?'

No answer was given.

Humphreys now decided to show Evans as a liar. He began thus:

'Now we will come back to the series of statements, and I am putting to you the general proposition that you are a man who is prepared to lie, if necessary upon oath, for your own convenience?'

'Not for my own convenience'.

Humphreys then went through a number of statements which Evans had previously made and he had to admit that most of them were untrue. He asked further questions:

'Let us look a little further at what I suggest is your habit of lying to suit your convenience. You lied to the Christies, did you not, that your wife was away, and all the rest of it, did you not?'

'I lied to Mrs Christie, yes'.

'All right, you lied to Mrs Christie. You lied to your aunt down in Wales, Mrs Lynch, did you not?'

'Yes, Sir'.

...

'So you lied to Mrs Christie, your aunt, the police and to your boss?'

'Yes; I did it all on the advice of Mr Christie'.

'All on the advice of Mr Christie. That is a new one'.

...

'Now, you are the person who alleges that Mr Christie is the murderer in this case; can you suggest why he should have strangled your wife?'

'Well, he was home all day'.

'Can you suggest why he should have strangled your wife?'

'No, I cannot'.

'Can you suggest why he should have strangled your daughter two days later?'

'No.'

121

This concluded the case for the defence. Evans's credibility was in shreds and he was found guilty and sentenced to death.

Another, similar series is *Celebrated British Trials*, but this suffers from being very incomplete in the coverage of the trial and much of it is omitted or abbreviated so we only read what the editor believes are the 'highlights'.

There are also the Old Bailey Accounts, published accounts of trials. These are available online at Oldbaileyonline.com and cover the years 1674–1913. They provide accounts of almost 200,000 trials at this court in London – the equivalent of the assizes in other counties – including fraud, theft, assault, treason and murder. They can be searched for by name of anyone involved in the trials, including defendant and victim. The earlier trials related tend to be in narrative form but the later ones read more like the question and answer format which takes place at trials. The following example, from 1713, has a most unexpected conclusion:

John Daley and Jane Roberts of the parish of St. Gregory by St. Paul, were indicted for the breaking the House of Sarah Cross on the 13th of January [1713] last night, and stealing thence a Silver Tea Kettle and Lamp, value 20L [£20], 4 Silver Candlesticks, value 5L, a large quantity of other Plate; and Silk Gown and Petty Coat embroider'd with Gold, and other rich Cloaths and Linen. The Evidence swore, That Roberts being a servant to Mrs Cross, knock'd at the Door, and she let him in without asking, who was there; whereupon This Evidence and a Footboy went Up stairs out of the kitchen to see who it should be, and when they came, Daley ask'd for one Madam Cheney, who had been gone ever since 6 o'clock; and that they heard him speak to some body and say, Come; upon which another man came in, and they forc'd the two witnesses down into the kitchen where they gagg'd and bound them; and that while they were in that Condition, Roberts came and look'd upon 'em and went up stairs again. Afterwards, they heard a great Noise of breaking glass, and something tumbling down stairs, and then heard the Door shut; and when their Mistress came home, the men were gone with the Goods, and Roberts with them. It appear'd also, That Mrs Cross had the key of her Scrutore in which the plate was, and that they had broke the Glass-ds, as they had also some Trunks for the Cloaths; but it was not prov'd that the Chamber doors were lock'd. The Constable who took Daley upon suspicion, swore, that he confess'd the Matter when taken, and had him to a house in Grays-Inn-Passage, where he found the goods, and the Prisoner Roberts; and when they were brought before my Lord Mayor, they both confess'd, Daley saying that Roberts persuaded him to it; and she, that he made love to her, and drew her in. Daley had several Gentlemen to his Reputation, who said they never heard any ill of him before; and he would have deny'd his former Confession, saying he was in Drink; however, it was very plain they were both Guilty of Felony, but were acquitted of the Burglary.

PRIMARY SOURCES: CONTEMPORARY ACCOUNTS

Another source for crime history is the multi-volume *Newgate Calendar*, which can be seen online at www.exclassics.com/ewgate/mgintro.thm. The *Newgate Calendar* was named after the famous London prison of the same name which existed until 1902. At one time it was said to be the most popular book in the country after the Bible, with its grim accounts of terrible tales throughout Britain. There were six volumes published in 1774 with major reworking and additions in the 1820s. They included stories of highwaymen, robbers, cannibals, cruel mistresses, killers, sadistic smugglers, forgers and miscreants of all descriptions. They were a form of bloodthirsty entertainment which set out to shock, but were also often morality tales, with the villains almost always being arrested, tried and hanged. The books are opposed to Catholicism, drunkenness, prostitution, gambling, the French, the Commonwealth and supportive of the monarchy, the established church and law and order. Not all are true; the account of the sixteenth-century Scottish cannibal Sawney Beane is thought to be fictitious.

After detailing their crimes, the seventh volume relates the end of the lives of William Jackson and Thomas Bucknell, sentenced to death in 1804 for forgery. The narrative states:

These two unfortunate victims of the violated laws of their country were ordered for execution on Thursday, July 26, 1804; but, we are sorry to add, they did not meet their fate with that firmness and resignation which would have become them as men and Christians. When the inferior officers of justices attended to conduct them from their cell to the scaffold, they found both Jackson and Bucknell in a situation which too clearly indicated that they had attempted to destroy themselves. They had taken poison; but it was either not of sufficient virulence, or had not been administered in such a way as to destroy life. It only produced a sort of lethargy, but not to that degree as to prevent the unfortunate men from feeling the wretchedness into which their guilt had plunged them. They were obliged to be supported on the platform by the executioner and his assistants, who observed, that they had never seen men quit life with less courage. The weak state to which they had reduced themselves rendered their passage to eternity but of a short duration. They expired without a struggle; and, having been exposed the usual time, as an example to others, their bodies were delivered to their friends for that decent interment which, had their suicidal attempt succeeded, the rigour of law would have denied them.

Not all publications which dealt with crime were so low brow. Men and women often took to riot in hard economic times. *The Gentleman's Magazine*, which ran from 1731 to 1868 and can be viewed on Ancestry, often reported significant crime and public disorder. Alongside essays and poems, political comment and reviews, it also dealt with crime. Its 'Historical Chronicle', which appeared in each monthly edition, for July 1740 reported the following:

> On the 9th past, began a great Riot at Newcastle upon Tyne, on Account of the Dearness of Corn; the Militia being raised, and Mr Alderman Ridley promising the Rioters (after he had consulted the Factors) That they should have Corn at a much lower rate, they were pacify'd. Next day the factors set a price on their Grain, and declar'd that all who apply'd should have it at the Rate fixed: Of this the Alderman, at the Head of the Militia, gave notice to the Multitude, who received it with Satisfaction and Applause. On the 21st, the Pitmen, Keelmen, and all the Poor of the Town made Application for Corn at the price promised; but the Factors kept their shops shut, and most of them absconded for Fear; upon this the Mob plunder'd the Granaries. The next 3 days nothing material happen'd, but the Discovery of a Vessel going off with Rye, which was stopp'd, and some of the Grain sold to the Poor at the price fixed. On the 25th the Militia were imprudently disbanded, and the next Day the Rioters assembled on the Sands-Hill; upon which the Mayor, the above Alderman, and some other Gentlemen, met at the guildhall to consult. But the Mob growing more outrageous, the Aldermen proposed to defend ye Rye-Ship while the Poor were supply'd; this being agreed to, and the Gentlemen venturing among them to let them know it, was knock'd down and much wounded, which provoked some Gentlemen to fire; whereby one of the Rioters was killed and several dangerously wounded. The Rabble then fell upon the Gentlemen in the Hall, wounded most of them, ransack'd the Place, and the Court and Chambers, destroying the Public Writings and Accounts, and carried off near 1800l of the Town's Money. After this they patroll'd about the Streets, all the Shops being shut, and threaten'd to burn and destroy the whole Place; but in the Evening 3 Companies of Howard's regiment enter'd the Town and dispersed the Rioters, forty of which were committed.

Another good contemporary periodical which dealt with a variety of current events was the *Annual Register* which began life in 1758 and is still being published. Its Chronicle for April 1826 included the following piece:

4. ATROCIOUS ASSAULT – Samuel Gilbert Was found guilty at the Taunton assizes, of robbing Charlotte Smith. The conduct of the prisoner towards the prosecutrix surpassed in atrocity that of almost any person who had ever appeared at the bar of justice. Having enticed her to walk with him to his aunt's. He on the road attempted to violate her. She resisted; he threw her down, stamped upon her, and tore her clothes into strips: he then took her in his arms, and carried her to the river, threatening to throw her in if she would not comply with his desire: she begged for mercy; he then dragged her into a lane, threw her over a gate, and cast her into a muddy ditch; still he could not accomplish his purpose, owing to her determined resistance. He afterwards pressed her head into the mud, and nearly suffocated her, and would probably have done so, if he had not heard the barking of a dog; she then, hoping to get rid of him, feebly said, 'The lord be praised, here's my father!' when the prisoner tore off her pocket, forcibly pulled out her ear-rings, and ran away.

PRIMARY SOURCES: PUBLISHED ARCHIVES

Published primary sources are very useful, especially for the early modern period (sixteenth and seventeenth centuries) where the assize records can be lacking. Two major series are the Calendars of State Papers Domestic and the Acts of the Privy Council. The Calendars of State Papers Domestic are summaries of correspondence to the Secretaries of State from 1509 to 1704. The two Secretaries of State were among the most powerful members of the government and they dealt with a great bulk of correspondence on all matters of public policy and importance. Law and order loomed high in these concerns. These volumes each cover about one year and are arranged chronologically. They are also indexed by person and place.

In 1539 Sir John Huddylton corresponded with Thomas Cromwell, then Henry VIII's leading minister. One of Sir John's servants had been murdered in Cheltenham by Thomas Futman, Harry Pudsay and John Strathforth. The three had been apprehended, indicted for their crime and put in the town's gaol, but witnesses dared not testify and the three were released. Futman had sought sanctuary at Westminster.

The issue was first raised on 8 June, and in another volume Sir John laid out his case (28 October). This time he stated:

> I beg that one Thomas Foutman, who is in sanctuary, and indicted for the death of my servant, may suffer death for it. One Pudsay is also indicted for it, and removed into the King's Bench, that he may be saved, which were great pity. I beg to have a writ to send him down into this shire again that he may suffer here, for there is one Stratforthe who was the head of them all at the murder, and we cannot get him indicted, he is so borne by his master Sir John a Brggyes. After the murder Starthforthe went home and some persons with him, but cannot be found, they been in such confederacy. I desire to have a Privy Seal for Roland Morton and Richard Redes, justices, who let the murderers to bail contrary to law.

Regrettably that was the last we hear on this matter, so whether justice for Sir John's servant was achieved cannot be known.

The Privy Council was another organ of the state, being a group of ministers and others who met with the monarch from time to time. As with the Secretaries of State, they could also be appealed to from those in need in the country. Their Act Books from 1386 to 1680 have been calendared and these indexed volumes also contain appeals, some of which are in the form of petitions to deal with instances of injustice. Again, as with the Secretaries of State, outcomes are often unknown.

One piteous appeal was made on 21 June 1615 to the 'Lord Councell of Yorke' that was passed to the Privy Council.

By this inclosed Peticion yow may understand that complainte hath ben made unto us on the behalf of one Thomas Parlsow, a prisoner in that citty of York, of much wronge and oppression done unto him by one John Rushworth and others as well, in defeatinge him of a good estate of lands belonging to his auncestors in as now of late in molestinge and hindringe him by unjust imprisonment: in prosecuting the execution of a comisison graunted unto him out of His Majesty's Courte of wardes, for the finding of divers rentes and ther duties accrewing to is Majesty out of the said lands, which the peticioner informeth, are fraudently detained by the said Rishworth, together with many the particular practises mencioned in the peticion to the utter impoveryshinge of the poore man. And for as much as the peticoner hath indured two yeare's imprisonment, which as it deemth by his infirmity, proceeded from noe other grownds than his adversares' practice to stop the expence of the said commission, were one therefore pray and require your lordship etc., to call both parties before yow and to examine the truth of this complaint, and thereupon to order some such course for the poore man's reliefe and the finall endinge and determyninge of the difference between then as shall be agreeable to equity and god conscience. And soe wee bid, etc.

Although there are relatively few archives for those transported to America and the West Indies, a number of works have been published which shed light on the matter. Peter Wilson Coldham wrote *The Complete Book of Emigrants in Bondage, 1614–1775*. This is an alphabetical listing of men and women transported, as well as stating where they were tried. He also wrote a book, *Bonded Passengers to America*, which is a guide to sources held at TNA.

The published *State Papers Colonial* provide lists of transportees, by ship, giving the date of sailing, the destination, name of ship and master, as well as a list of transportees. Those guilty of treason were often transported, too. The major instances of this were following the defeats of the rebellions of 1685, 1715 and 1745. Covering the Monmouth Rebellion are various books: an edition of the *Notable British Trials*, *The Bloody Assizes, Monmouth's Rebels* by W M Wigfield and published by the Somerset Record Society in 1985. There is no one book listing the prisoners and their fates following the Jacobite Rebellion of 1715, but Margaret Sankey's book, *Punishing Rebellion* (2005) provides an overview. English prisoners are dealt with by Leo Gooch in *The Desperate Faction* (1995) and Jonathan Oates in *Preston: The Last Battle on English Soil* (2015) which also covers rioters in the north-west of England in 1715. The most comprehensive account of the Jacobite prisoners of the 1745 rebellion – more than 3,000 of them – is the three volumes of the *Scottish Historical Society* (3rd series, vols. 13–15, published in 1928–9).

MEMOIRS AND DIARIES

Criminals, journalists, police officers, pathologists, coroners, magistrates, victims and many others associated with crime write memoirs for publication. These can be very useful sources from one point of view, i.e. the view of the author, though they will inevitably be biased as is the case with all memoirs and autobiographies. Thus books written by former criminals will underplay the author's criminality, suggesting that victims were far from innocent and that the agents of the law were corrupt/violent. The books also will tend to focus on well-known crimes. So there are numerous books by the Great Train Robbers of 1963 and police officers will write about well-known offences that they dealt with, so ex-Superintendent John Du Rose wrote about the Thames Nudes Murders of 1964–5 and in particular his role in bringing the murders to an end (highly disputed by some crime historians) in *Murder was My Business*, as well as his dealings with the Krays and John Haigh. Ex-Chief Inspector Dew focused on Jack the Ripper and Dr Crippen in *I Caught Crippen*.

Du Rose later recalled in his memoirs an interview he had with acid bath killer, John Haigh:

> He gave apparently straightforward answers to all our questions and nothing he said could be challenged … The three of us sat in such a way as to form a triangle, so that I was watching Haigh's profile during Webb's questioning, and Webb was watching his face and neck from the same angle when I put the questions. Thus we both noticed the very odd behaviour of his adam's apple. Every time he answered a question he gulped to swallow saliva and his adam's apple seemed to be flying up and down like a yo yo … The rapid action of his adam's apple was not normal. It was an involuntary physical reaction bred of nervous tension while we were questioning him, and it clearly indicated that the man had nothing on his conscience.

Chief Inspector Wensley provided accounts of some of his cases from the late Victorian era to the 1920s, published as *Detective Days* in 1931. He describes his first encounter with Edith Thompson, charged as being partly responsible for her husband's murder by her lover Bywaters:

> There was no doubt that her distress was genuine. I saw she could scarcely have been called a pretty woman, but she had a distinctly attractive personality. She carried herself well, was dressed tastefully – she still wore the evening gown in which she had gone to the theatre and spoke with an air of culture. In moments of animation she must have been a woman of considerable fascination. Even seeing her as I did at this original interview, when she was under great stress of mind, she impressed me as being normally a woman above the average intelligence.

Pathologists such as Dr Keith Simpson include cases such as

James Hanratty, Lord Lucan, John Christie and others. Dr Simpson was a veteran pathologist and when he published his memoirs, *Forty Years of Murder*, in 1978 it became a best-seller. He included much information about his post-mortems, courtroom exchanges and more general information about the cases which surrounded them. His writing is often graphic and not for the squeamish, but will be crucial for researchers into a particular crime. During the Second World War the doctor had to deal with the corpse of Leonard Moules and he described the examination thus:

> His scalp had been split by five successive blows with a blunt instrument of moderate weight. Four of the injuries were set close together and parallel to one another: this suggested to me that these blows had been struck when the old man was already incapable of resisting or moving, or perhaps when his head was being held steady for the purpose; and deep bruising of the neck muscles did, in fact, indicate that the neck had at some point been gripped strongly by a left hand. The fifth injury lay apart, being set in a different place and at a different angle. It was distinctly heavier than the others and I thought it would have been sufficient to disable the victim, although not, perhaps, to knock him out completely. It could well have been delivered as Moules approached with his head slightly bent forward, and I thought it quite likely that this disabling injury had been the first. If I was right, old Moules had been knocked out and then deliberately and cold-bloodedly battered to death.

Nasty stuff. However, as with all evidence, we must be careful not to treat it all as being wholly accurate. Dr Simpson in another chapter describes a victim (Margery Gardner, murdered by Neville Heath in 1946) whom he examined. Whilst his examination should not be doubted, as, after all, he was personally involved, he then perhaps oversteps the mark and writes about the character of a victim, which he only knew through hearsay. He introduces her as 'married, attractive and promiscuous', a mix of fact and opinion. But he then goes on to report

> Had she allowed him to tie her up? Probably she had; it came out later that Margery Gardner was a masochist. She liked being bound and lashed. She had gone to Heath's room for pleasurable flagellation, and that may have been all he intended to give her when she offered her naked body to his whip. But she must have known the danger. Indeed, according to J.D. Casswell, KC … 'It is almost certain … that a month before her death she had been with Heath to another hotel bedroom and had only been saved by the timely intervention by a hotel detective. She had been heavily thrashed and Heath was standing over her.'

Casswell and Simpson got this wrong. Inspection of the files of the police investigation showed that the woman saved from Heath was not Margery Gardner. The police also questioned Margery's husband and other men who knew her. None referred to her having any masochistic tastes. Regrettably others writing about this case have copied Simpson's remarks and thus perpetuated myths about the unfortunate woman.

Victims who do survive sometimes discuss their lives, their ordeals and the aftermath of such terrible experiences in print, for example Jill Seward in *Rape: My Story* about her ordeal when she was attacked in her father's Ealing Vicarage in 1986. Survivors' stories of sexual assaults can be extremely harrowing for the reader and there are numerous 'misery memoirs', which also include stories of people who have survived serial killers or whose relative has fallen victim to one. Books of reminiscences by the young women who suffered from the Wests in Gloucester but who escaped to tell the tale are recent examples of this.

Diaries and memoirs can often provide insights into the experiences of victims, but only if those victims are literate and articulate. John Evelyn was attacked whilst riding alone in Kent in

1654 and later recounted what happened when he was surprised by two robbers:

> striking with their long staves at the horse, taking hold of the reignes, threw me downe, & immediately tooke my sword, & haled me into a deepe Thickett, some quarter of a mile from the high-way, where they might securely rob me, as they soone did; what they got of mony was not considerable, but they took two rings, the one an Emrald with diamonds, an (Onyx), & a pair of boucles set with rubies & diamonds which were of value, and after all, barbrously bound my hands behind me, & my feete, having before pull'd off my bootes: & then set me up against an Oake, with most bloudy threatening to cut my throat, if I offerd to crie out, or make any noise, for that they should be within hearing, I not being the person they looked for: I told them, if they had not basely surpriz'd me, they should not have made so easy a prize ... at which they cock'd their pistols, & told me they had long guns too, & were 14 companions, which all were lies.

Evelyn later managed to untie himself and recovered some of his property.

Alexander Kay Goodlet's unpublished diary for 21 May 1934 records his being attacked in the street in Ealing:

> After dinner took the Boys to the fair and then went to Lyons. Found Stanley here when I returned; and it was when escorting him home that the fun started. We were accosted at the head of Granville Gardens by 4 or 5 young toughs, who descended from insults to blows, I getting a beauty on the jaw. I gave the lout a fair biff with my stick and they hauled off; but five minutes later up he came and certainly gave me a pasting, breaking my pipe in my mouth and giving me a rotten cut in the roof of my palate. I did not retaliate, not wanting to be

mixed up in a scrap with my glasses; how the swine didn't knock them off I don't know. Stanley was forcing me away when up came the police and I charged the whole lot of them. What a dressing down both the officers gave them. Eventually I said I would not prefer a charge and the police sent them about their business. And so the episode closed; but I've a mouth that hurts like hell. I'm really sorry that I wear glasses and am afraid (legally) about being mixed up in rows, as I'm glad to find that I remain quite calm and cold even in the midst of a racket like that.

Many of our criminal ancestors will have spent time in prison. There are plenty of memoirs which concern life in prison by literate inmates. If your ancestor spent time in one of the same gaols at the same time as one of these people, they would certainly be worth reading to gain an insight into life at that institution at that time.

Peter Wildeblood was a well-educated man who found himself in Wormwood Scrubs Prison in 1950, having been found guilty of homosexual offences. Unusually among prisoners he wrote a great deal about his experiences in prison which were published thereafter (in *Against the Law*, 1955). He described it as being 'a huge extravagantly architected place of dingy brick and grubby stone'. When in prison he was forced to wear the coarse grey prison uniforms. He had starchy, dull foods to eat. One example was fried fish, cabbage, potatoes and pudding, to be eaten out of a single deep tin with a spoon. His life would be regimented and controlled as never before; a bath day, a day to return library books, a pay day and church on Sundays. Wildeblood commented on life for an inmate there in the early 1950s that it was a 'powerful shock. Suddenly in the space of a few hours, a man's whole life is changed.' He considered it to be 'the worst place to which a first offender can be sent, and that its sanitary conditions would … disgrace a Hottentot village'. In the prison workshops where he would be employed there was no talking among prisoners. At that time birching in prison was still legal, though there's no evidence that Wildeblood was ever disciplined in such a fashion. Prison was not a pleasant experience.

Charles Bronson, a violent and prolific criminal, wrote *The Good Prison Guide* after having experienced a number of prisons in the late twentieth century and Reg Kray included chapters in his autobiography, *My Story*, about his time in various places of incarceration such as Parkhurst and then Broadmoor. Bronson also wrote a book about his time in Broadmoor, describing it and its staff as being hell on earth (Kray had a less extreme version of his time there and details the routine of his arrival and his daily activities). He also writes about his attempts to beat the system by climbing onto the roof and hurling missiles at the staff below. High-profile prisoners, such as the novelist Jeffrey Archer, have written about prison life. There have also been memoirs about life in young offenders' institutions, such as Brendan Behan's *Borstal Boy*, written in 1958 about his time in a borstal at Hollesley Bay thirty years previously.

Prison reformers have also written accounts of prisons in order to influence governments to liberalise penal policy. These include works by Elizabeth Fry (1780–1845), a Quaker prison reformer, such as *Prisons in Scotland and the North of England*. She not only visited but also stayed the night in prisons as a guest. How reliable these are is another question, for clearly they were written with a purpose in mind.

These books may be of use when the writer discusses less well-known crimes, such as minor thefts or similar which they were involved in as a prelude to the famous crimes. They can give an insight into the mentality of criminals and how they justify their actions to themselves and to the public, and what they think about other villains. Reginald Kray in *My Story* writes about other criminals he met in Broadmoor and elsewhere. Police officers' insights into crime can also be revealing, but where a criminal is unidentified, there is often no consensus. For example, several police memoirs discuss the Ripper case, but they suggest different solutions to this great unsolved mystery.

SECONDARY SOURCES

Books about crime by those who are not direct participants are very common. Some appear very soon after the events in question, often written by journalists. They can capture the immediacy of events and personalities and use local colour and recreate the atmosphere of the times. They can also talk to some of those intimately involved; David Briffett, who wrote *The Acid Bath Murders*, had the advantage of being able to talk to a police officer and a pathologist directly involved in the case, which a current historian cannot do as both are now deceased. However they are based on limited sources as documents used by police or courts are usually not instantly available and so vital pieces of evidence may not be included. Authors may be prejudiced in favour or against the key personalities involved in the crime and may be moralistic. The same can be said of newspaper accounts, too.

These books tend to focus on the criminal rather than the victims. Thus Molly Lefebure, writing *Murder with a Difference* in 1958 about Christie and Haigh, has lots to write about the killers, but all we know about the family that the latter slew is as follows:

> The amusement arcade [which Haigh briefly managed] was owned and run by an elderly Scot named William Donald McSwan and his son, a young man of Haigh's own age, young Donald, known to his friends as 'Mac' ... Old Mr McSwan (now over seventy), although living frugally on a Local Government pension, had money invested ... Mac, to use his more familiar name, would sometimes meet Haigh for a drink at midday, sometimes in the evening for supper.

John Williams in *Hume: Portrait of a Double Murderer*, published in 1960, spends a chapter discussing Hume's alleged first victim, but the second is dismissed thus: 'Fifty year old taxi driver, Arthur Maag'. Books can also denigrate the character of a victim; Ludovic Kennedy in *Ten Rillington Place* is scathing about Ethel Christie (murdered by her husband), 'naïve, passive, homely, not outwardly

136

attractive' and 'gullible enough to believe anything that anyone told her'. No evidence is given for any of this, but the author states it as fact because this suits the case he is building up against her husband as being the killer of fellow tenants Beryl and Geraldine Evans (another author suggests that Mrs Christie was anything but a fool, in order to then suggest that her husband did not kill the Evanses). Kennedy also refers to an unnamed woman whom Christie once lived with as being 'a prostitute' (the detailed newspaper report about it names her with no indication that she was a prostitute). Another author referring to a case where a young woman was killed after going off on a beach with two men previously unknown to her suggests that her murder was partly her own fault:

> Irene Munro's story might well be called 'A Warning to Wantons'. The girl's incredible folly at first detracts from any sympathy felt for her. In defence of it one can only plead her youth, her early years overshadowed by the war, the emancipation which women were just then beginning to experience and enjoy, her loneliness in strange place, and her undoubted weakness for the opposite sex. Certain medical pronouncements proved that she must have been over sexed and slightly abnormal.

Then there are those accounts written long after the events they describe which means that the author is often able to draw on materials not available to the general public at the time of the events being described. Police and judicial files are usually closed for decades after a crime has taken place and so the author writing at the time of a crime has no access to them. The 'True Crime' genre has boomed in the twentieth century. Most bookshops will have a whole section devoted to it. Generally speaking they fall into two main categories. Those devoted to specific crimes or criminals and those which cover a number of crimes, perhaps categorised by type of offence/offender or by district. There are many of the latter, often organised by town/city or by county.

The first type of books varies considerably in quality. Clearly those which deal with one crime or one criminal should be able to write in great detail about their subject, drawing on many of the sources already referred to in this book and have something original to tell on the topic. They also should be well illustrated and include a bibliography of sources which may be of use to the reader as the book is unlikely to have exhausted each one. The substance of the book as well as its size will vary and some authors insist on including every scrap of information they find in their research and may well want to add a very significant amount of contextualisation and comparative matter. Others are more concise. For instance a recent book about Dr Crippen has nothing to say about the role of women on stage in the Edwardian period or of quack doctors at the time (Mrs Crippen was an amateur artiste and her husband dealt with alternative medicines). The popular *Suspicions of Mr Whicher* about the Road House Murder of 1860 is vastly expanded by the author's lengthy dissertations on the birth and role of the Detective Force and Victorian novelists such as Wilkie Collins.

Books about particularly infamous crimes have a tendency to repeat established myths about the case, unless the author, be it Philip Sugden writing about the Ripper murders or Jonathan Oates writing about the Christie killings, has taken the trouble to consult contemporary material, paying close heed to archive sources and other eye-witness testimonies. In fact there is more hard fact available about the victims of the Ripper than the man himself – about whose identity there is a great deal of speculation.

There are some publishers who have had whole series of books which aim to cover numerous instances of serious crime, almost always murder. Pen and Sword commissioned many *Foul Deeds and Suspicious Deaths* books and so have other publishers, often arranged by town or county. These contain a number of chapters, each dealing with one particular crime or criminal. Their advantage is that they each cover at least a dozen or more cases, but their disadvantage is that each is covered relatively thinly and only a very small portion of the information that is available is used therein. Often they tend

The Author with one of his books. Author's wife

to repeat what has been written in other books (history does not repeat itself but historians do) because it is very difficult to research each case in the same depth as if one were just writing about one case. In the otherwise excellent *Murder Houses of Greater London*, Dr Bondeson's treatment of the Hume case suggests that the author believes the testimony of the killer (a known liar and fantasist) is truthful as it is passed off as fact.

Finally, the researcher may want to 'read around the topic' as history teachers at A-level and university lecturers are forever (optimistically) exhorting their students to do. This basically means to try reading books about the environs, both physical and social, of the location of the crime in question. Did the offence take place in an affluent neighbourhood or was it in a slum (more likely)? There are local history books about all Britain's towns and cities and about most of its villages, too. These may well help to provide some of the answers. General accounts of crime in academic studies may also be useful for context, especially in the case of where crime has a political dimension, where the miscreants are Jacobites, Jacobins, Luddites, Suffragettes, Fascists or Communists. These will help explain the motivation of the people involved, what the responses of those in authority and the general public were, and the ultimate significance of their movement in history.

Care needs to be taken when dealing with books for several reasons. First, the author may well have an axe to grind (a criminal author may well be virulently opposed to the agents of law and order) or may have a political point to make, as with Ludovic Kennedy in *Ten Rillington Place* where he is obsessed with proving that Timothy Evans was innocent of the murders for which he was hanged. Research is very variable and writing skills likewise. What any book cannot be, however, is the final word on the subject. Often the bibliography, if there is one, can be the best part of the book for it will list sources used and these may include ones that a researcher was unaware of and may want to locate. Books which have footnotes are even more useful as they will provide the actual source of each piece of information (assuming the footnotes are correct – those in E P Thompson's *Whigs and Hunters*, about eighteenth-century poachers, were not always so but the staff at Hampshire Record Office were able to locate the appropriate documents for this author).

Books inevitably focus on well-known crimes and criminals: the Great Train Robbers, Jack the Ripper, Ruth Ellis, Dr Crippen and so on. They do not focus on the majority of criminals whose deeds are relatively petty and in any case there would be insufficient material to write a book about a lad who got into trouble for stealing apples or a sheep stealer sent to Australia. Books which are collections of primary material, such as trials, State Papers and Privy Council Acts, as well as contemporary books which include statements about crime, may well be of more use than those books available in the 'true crime' sections of bookshops. The majority of these books can be accessed by visiting the British Library, for which a reader's ticket is needed, but many may be available from online book shops and libraries.

Chapter 7

OTHER SOURCES

This book has already covered many of the sources useful for those investigating their criminal and victim ancestors. There are a variety of other sources of information, too; some of which you might need to investigate, others not. Furthermore, not all will be relevant for all crimes, but some will.

CORONERS' INQUESTS

Since 1194 coroners have been charged with investigating suspicious deaths by holding an inquest. Until 1926 the coroner did not have to have any medical or legal qualifications, though many had. A jury was also required and in the country inquests were often held in the upper room of a public house, this being the only room large enough to gather so many people together. Juries were also required to see the corpse. 'Suspicious deaths' are not merely murders and manslaughter, but are more commonly accidents, suicides (these were criminal offences up to 1961) and deaths in prison, including, perhaps bizarrely, executions, as in the latter case the cause of death is surely obvious. They tend not to include deaths by enemy action in wartime (except civilian deaths in the First World War). Until 1974 an inquest had the authority to name a suspect in a murder case if the evidence led in one particular direction. The last inquest to do so was that held in London in 1974 following the murder of Sandra Rivett, Lord Lucan being named as the culprit. Coroners have diverse jurisdictions; some cover a county, some a city and others part of a county.

A sixteenth-century Sussex inquest was recorded thus:

24 September 1539 Laughton

Stephen Rote, county coroner. Jurors: John Wynam, John Combes, John Holybon, John Davy, Thomas Lye, John Hooke, George Weller, Lawrence Peckam, John Wood of Bull, John Averey, Thomas Terrey, John Bery. About 11pm on 3 September, when Thomas Edson late of Laughton, servant of Nicholas Pellam, esq., and keeper of his deer in Vert wood in Laughton, was walking in Vert Wood with others to guard the deer, Robert Kent assaulted him and they fought together. While they were fighting, Edson, to defend both himself and his master's deer, killed Kent in self defence and by mischance with a staff worth 2d which he held in both hands, giving him a mortal wound on the head to the brain.

Until recently inquests were held a day or two after the corpse was located, but were often adjourned and not concluded until weeks or months later. In some cases it can now be years later. Most coroners' records are held in county record offices. Until 1921 there was no requirement to keep them. From 1921 they were to be kept but of course many had already been destroyed. Those created after about 1875 do not survive in their entirety. What does survive can be quite patchy, as there is no obligation to keep all these records and so they have often been weeded. For example, the inquests on Christie's six victims (held at the London Metropolitan Archives) are often just one page with very basic details recorded there of name, cause of death and not much else. Yet for his first victim, Ruth Fuerst, murdered in 1943, there is a comprehensive list of her many occupations and addresses from her arrival In England in 1939 to her last job four years later. This information can be found nowhere else. For his fourth victim Kathleen Maloney, murdered in 1953, there is correspondence from one of her five children and journalist Ludovic Kennedy about the case.

Inquest records are often closed for seventy-five years from the date of their being held, in the name of the Data Protection Act, but this does not seem to have been a hard and fast rule. The author recalls seeing the inquest record of John Haigh, hanged in Wandsworth Prison in 1949, a mere sixty-four years after the event, but when asking about that held in the same year in Chelmsford for car dealer Stanley Setty was told that it was closed until 2025.

Some records are held at TNA. A handful of inquest records which raised particular issues of wider public concern, such as disease in prison or a military suicide, are held there and can be found by searching the website.

Some inquests held for prisoners dying behind bars are held here, too. Debtors and others held at the King's Bench prison from 1747–50 and 1771–1839 can be seen in KB14. They record prisoners with details of previous occupations. Those dying at the Millbank Penitentiary from 1848 to 1863 had their inquest records held at PCOM2/165. Records of those prisoners held by the order of the High Court of Admiralty or who had drowned in the Thames can be found for 1535–1688 in HCA1/78–84 and for 1816–32 in HCA1/86 and 102–9.

Inquests are also often reported in the press and sometimes this may be the best account of them; see Chapter 5 for a discussion of material held by newspapers. Some inquests have been published by the ever useful county record societies. For example, R F Hunniset has published Sussex Coroners' records from 1485–1688 in four volumes (1985–98) and those for Wiltshire from 1752–96. Bedfordshire Coroners' Rolls from 1265 to 1380 have also been published, as have medieval coroners' rolls for Lancashire (1205–1307, 1310–55) and Buckinghamshire (1373–91).

Ingleby Oddie was coroner for Westminster in the early twentieth century and in 1941 he published a book of his reminiscences, titled *Inquest*, including the famous cases he had been involved in, and his comments upon them. It will be of interest to those who want to learn how a coroner went about his work at that time. The key guide to coroners' records is Jeremy Gibson and Colin Rogers's *Coroners' Records in England and Wales*, 3rd edition (2009), as this gives an alphabetical listing, county by county, as to what survives and its location.

In Ireland those coroners' records for the nineteenth and twentieth centuries which survived the great record office fire of 1922 are now held at the National Archives of Ireland in Dublin. The Public Record Office of Northern Ireland in Belfast has many coroners' records since 1872. Those from 1872 to 1920 have been indexed and the latter can be searched at www.proni.gov.uk. The originals can be seen at the PRO for Northern Ireland.

There are no coroners or inquests in Scotland. All suspicious deaths are dealt with by the Procurator Fiscal, a Crown official, to whom they are reported. He must then investigate and if he finds it necessary, there will be a further investigation, though this may take place weeks or months later, whereas in England or Wales an inquest will be days later. In the case of the apparent suicide of Bertha Merrett in Edinburgh in 1926 it was some months before a correspondence began between the Procurator Fiscal and others as to whether this was murder and the chief suspect arrested.

STATE PAPERS DOMESTIC AND STATE PAPERS SCOTLAND

From 1509 to 1782 the Secretaries of State were responsible for much of domestic and foreign policy and in the former role had much to do in cases pertaining to law and order and would correspond with magistrates, judges, merchants, soldiers and others. State Papers Domestic deal largely with English concerns and those for Scotland naturally deal with affairs north of the border. The in-letters would be addressed to the Secretary and would provide information or perhaps make requests. They have been calendared and indexed from 1509 to 1704.

State Papers Domestic (SPD) are a number of series divided by reign; hence State Papers Domestic for George I are SPD35 and those for his successor, George II, SPD36. Their survival is various; those for the early years of George I are sparse indeed compared to those for his successor's reign. There are also additional series, such as SP44 Letter books, which comprise further sets of letters. These archives are unindexed, so without a rough idea of the date, searching is a lengthy task.

VISITS

Fieldwork is always an important part of research, if it is at all possible. It is not necessary to commit a crime nor to become a prison officer to visit a prison. When I was researching the biography of a serial killer, I contacted the governor of Wandsworth Prison where he was incarcerated prior to his execution in 1949. A date was arranged and I went to the grim edifice in south London, a place I had never seen before. It is certainly not somewhere to visit for pleasure. On arrival at the main gate, I explained my purpose and all electronic devices (telephone and camera) had to be handed in at that point.

I was then in the company of a group of nurses from a nearby hospital and a prison officer who was also in charge of the small prison museum. He showed us around the place, including into the former condemned cell and adjacent execution room, the chapel and

Wandsworth Prison. Author's collection

the yard, including a note of where remains of the executed are (in unmarked graves under concrete). We walked around the corridors and I was rather unnerved to see others passing us by – these were prisoners there (I had hitherto believed prisoners who were not engaged in activities were locked in cells). The sound of doors being locked and unlocked was frequent, but in a way the atmosphere was not as claustrophobic as it must be for the inmates as we knew that in a couple of hours we would be outside again.

As an experience for a historian with an interest in a former inmate it was a worthwhile exercise, and those with criminal ancestors might well want to visit the place where their ancestor was held. Whether permission will be granted is another question, but surely the question is worth asking on the basis of nothing ventured nothing gained. It should also be worth remembering that a prison, like any working building is not a static museum piece but a constantly evolving organism as conditions in prisons have altered throughout the years.

Up to 1964 those executed in prisons were buried on the site, usually in the yard and in unconsecrated ground. No gravestones or other markers were erected and when executions ceased the ground was concreted over. There is now no obvious place where the remains of killers and traitors remain. However, from 1965, the families of the deceased were permitted to have the remains transferred to consecrated ground in a cemetery or graveyard. The families of Ruth Ellis and Timothy Evans did so.

Some prisons which have been closed have been converted for other uses. Oxford Prison, part of Oxford Castle, closed in 1996. It is now in part a museum, which visitors can pay to be shown around by a costumed guide. This includes visits to rooms once used as cells. Another part of the prison is now a hotel and former cells are rooms for paying guests.

Other buildings once used for the purpose of justice can be visited. The former court house at Horsham in which the initial hearings for the case of the Crown versus John Haigh in 1949 took place is now a restaurant. If the place is relatively quiet the staff may

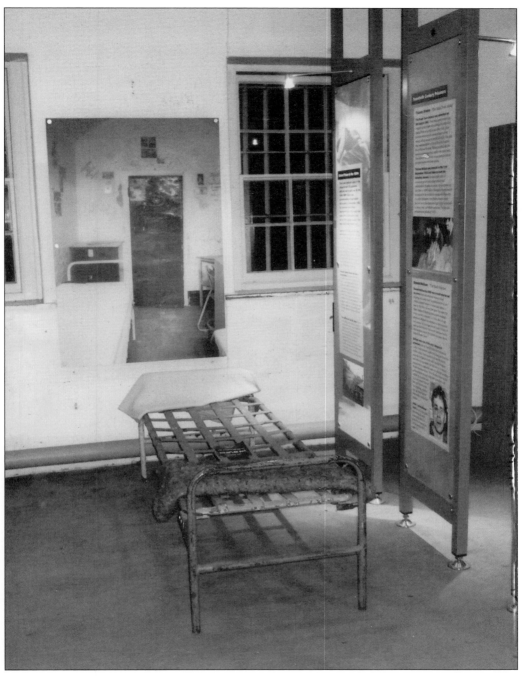

Interior of Oxford Prison Museum. The Author

Cell door at old Horsham Police Station. The Author

be able to show anyone interested the cells below. Nearby, at the town museum, the door to the police cell in the former police station can be seen and, if the peep hole is opened, the photograph of the face of a charming killer will be seen – the museum also has his comb, given to a member of staff by the said villain for whom grooming was very important. However, some former court houses have been converted into flats such as West London Magistrates' Court and Acton Court, both in west London.

Museums often include a few implements which deal with justice. The most obvious one is the one founded in the late nineteenth century and once named the Black Museum (now called the Crime Museum). It was once located in Scotland Yard and was only open to police and Home Office personnel and other special visitors – including bona-fide crime historians. Some exhibits were recently on public display in a temporary display at the Museum of London, but its future is currently uncertain because Scotland Yard has been sold.

The museum has an extremely impressive collection of items collected in the course of investigations into crime. It is certainly not for the squeamish. They include death masks of some of the hanged, together with nooses, as well as weapons used to commit crime, such as Ronald Chesney's handgun and, worse, the cooking implements used by Denis Nilsen to dismember his victims in the 1970s and 1980s. Other items associated with crime are there, such as devices employed by terrorists and kidnappers. Local museums may exhibit items pertaining to punishment and even torture. The Tower of London certainly has some of the latter.

CHURCHYARDS AND CEMETERIES

Other places to visit are the final earthly resting place of villains and victims. The remains of some criminals rest in churchyards or cemeteries, as do murder victims. Gravestones for killers will not make any reference to their former crimes (Timothy Evans's grave in Leytonstone Cemetery merely states his name and dates of birth and death). Those hanged for other offences may well refer to these

Gibbet Hill. From the Original picture at the "Royal Huts" Hotel, Hindhead.

Placed in chains, and there close by	Hanging there both night and day,
The London Road to be hung on high,	Till piece by piece they dropped away ;
Where travellers by coach or van	And on the spot where the foul deed was done,
All hear the tale of the murdered man,	Can now be seen by everyone,
As they near the gibbet tree—	And on that spot the travellers know
A sight more loathsome none could see.	No heath nor grass doth ever grow.

Gibbet Hill. Paul Lang's Collection

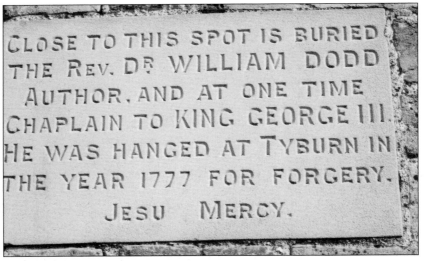

Memorial Plaque to Dr Dodd. The Author.

misdeeds, however. On the exterior wall of St Lawrence's church in Cowley, Middlesex, there is a plaque to the vicar's brother, Dr William Dodd, who was hanged after being found guilty of forging a bond for £4,200 in 1777.

Memorials to victims may well refer to their demise. For instance in Denham churchyard there is a concise summary of a terrible mass murder:

BENEATH THIS STONE LIE THE REMAINS OF
EMANUEL MARSHALL, AND CHARLOTTE, HIS WIFE,
ALSO MARY ANN, HIS SISTER,
AND MARY, THIRZA AND GERTRUDE HIS CHILDREN,
WHO TOGETHER WITH HIS MOTHER MARY MARSHALL,
WERE ALL BARBAROUSLY MURDERED ON SUNDAY
MORNING MAY 22ND 1870
BY JOHN OWENS, A TRAVELLING BLACKSMITH,
WHO WAS EXECUTED IN THE COUNTY GAOL AT
AYLESBURY AUGUST 8TH 1870

MARY	EMANUEL	MARY ANN
AGED 8 YEARS	AGED 35 YEARS	AGED 32 YEARS
THIRZA	CHARLOTTE	GERTRUDE
AGED 6 YEARS	AGED 34 YEARS	AGED 4 YEARS

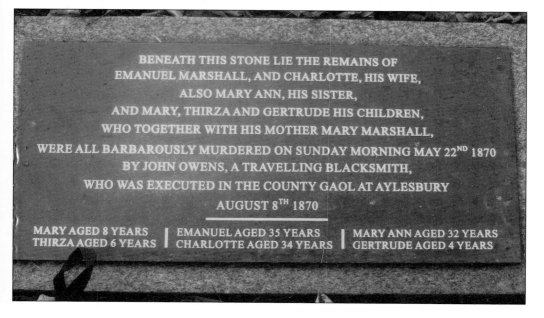

Such explicit reference to crime does not always happen, so the grave in the Golders Green Jewish Cemetery of a man who was stabbed to death and then dismembered so that only his torso could be located states:

IN
LOVING MEMORY
OF
STANLEY SETTY
WHO DIED
4TH OCTOBER 1949
DEEPLY MOURNED BY HIS SISTER, BROTHERS,
RELATIVES AND FRIENDS

Graves are not always easy to find in among hundreds or thousands of others, so it is essential to contact the cemetery authorities in advance – often the cemetery department of the council whose jurisdiction covers the cemetery. They will usually have a plan as to where all the graves are located and should be able to tell the enquirer what the location is, though there may be a fee for this. They should also have grave registers which will tell when the burial took place. Cemeteries are usually arranged systematically with rows and then numbered graves.

This is not always a guarantee of being able to find it; when looking for the grave of Bertha Merrett at Piershill Cemetery in Edinburgh, armed with the plot number, I found that there were no markers on the site to enable anyone to find it apart from looking at each stone; which is what I did and was successful, though in part this was because I had already seen a picture in a magazine of the unusual gravestone in question. What I could have done, if unsuccessful, was enquire at the cemeteries office to ascertain if there was a map showing grave plots.

Of course many buried bodies do not have gravestones, which, after all, cost money. Many poor victims from poor families may not have been able to afford them, but it is a very variable matter. Beryl and Geraldine Evans are commemorated on a gravestone, along with an unrelated individual, but fellow murder victims Rita Nelson and Kathleen Maloney, who are buried in the same cemetery (Gunnersbury, in west London), have their graves unmarked. Most burials take place in a cemetery in the same local government district where death occurred; though not necessarily, for some are buried in family plots which may be many miles away.

If you do not know in which cemetery someone is buried, try websites such as Find a Grave (www.findagrave.com), which may be useful, showing pictures of the person when alive, their grave, its location and other relevant details. The site is of course far from complete, but contains 150 million names (many of them in the USA and elsewhere), so may be worth checking.

Other useful websites are as follows. The National Burial Index is an excellent, though incomplete database of cemetery records in

Plaque to victims at Dunblane Cathedral. The Author.

the British Isles and can be searched on FindmyPast. Nineteenth-century Kent gravestones inscriptions can be seen at http://www.kentarchaeology.org.uk/Research/research.htm. Other useful sites are www.deceasedonline.com, www.worldburialindex.com, www.gravestonephotos.com, www.billiongraves.com. These websites often include additional information; transcripts of gravestones, photographs, location and other details.

Cemeteries did not exist until the middle of the nineteenth century or even later in rural districts, so burials would take place in churchyards. Very few people before the twentieth century are marked by gravestones unless they were of some standing or wealth. They are also organised in a more haphazard fashion. The gravestones in many churchyards have been indexed by the local family history society and these volumes can often be consulted online, by application to the said society or the local record office.

SCENES OF THE CRIME

It may also be interesting to visit where a crime involving one of your ancestors took place, if that place still exists. Dr Jan Bondeson's *Murder Houses* trilogy, published in 2014–15 is a gazetteer of houses in Greater London where murders took place and which houses still stand and so is a very useful guide. As to lesser offences and murders outside the capital, a visit may be needed. If the buildings/streets have been demolished or have been altered out of all recognition, it may be possible to obtain old postcards or photographs of the scenes in question.

Police stations, as well as court houses and prisons should also be on one's itinerary. Again, many have been demolished/rebuilt or are now used for other purposes, and will certainly be different internally. But since most criminal investigations were conducted at police stations, where crimes were reported and suspects held, they are worth a look to retrace the steps taken by your ancestor in their often lengthy journey from crime to justice. Bear in mind, though, that these are working buildings, not museums.

The list of places to visit could include many other places

associated with the crime in question, such as restaurants, cafes, pubs and hotels that have a bearing on the case. They may well still exist.

FILM AND TELEVISION

Real crimes have been portrayed on film and television and on the internet. These include dramatised versions, which should be seen as suspect because they are primarily drama, to be seen as entertainment. Documentaries should contain a number of people whose knowledge of the crime/s are thought to be significant, such as crime historians and former police officers, criminals, psychiatrists, academics, lawyers and pathologists. Some can be highly inaccurate, including at least two in Fred Dinenage's 'Notorious Criminal' series and some can be very sketchy such as those in the History Channel's 'Crime' series (allotting about six minutes to each case under review). They should not be wholly dismissed, because they may include witnesses offering testimony which may be new.

Dramas tend to stick to famous and infamous crimes and criminals and often focus on the criminal rather than the victim/s. For example, in *A is for Acid*, a 2002 TV film about the killings of John George Haigh in the 1940s very little attention is paid to the victims (or the killer's motivation/psychology). *Dance with a Stranger*, about Ruth Ellis, does not show her shooting an innocent bystander as well as her lover in 1955 and neglects her earlier life. The 1970s TV series *Dick Turpin* and (needless to say) *Carry on Dick* are figments of pure fantasy with the robber/murderer/rapist being a romantic hero and friend of the poor. Or some films aim to portray a particular crime as a miscarriage of justice (*10 Rillington Place* and *Give it to him, Chris*) and are arguably propaganda films where truth is at a premium. The various films on Jack the Ripper are rather fictional, too; in one, *Murder by Decree* (1965), all the victims are all young and attractive women whereas in reality this was not the case.

Rather more strongly based on reality were the courtroom dramas *Ladykillers*, broadcast in 1979–80. Covering over a dozen notorious trials (six male and six female defendants) from the nineteenth century to the 1950s they give a simplified impression about trials at the Old Bailey in these decades, but at least show the examination and cross-examination of witnesses and the interventions of the judge.

Explicitly fictional films or TV series can help give an impression about crime, criminals and victims – and how society viewed them – and can be instructive. The Ealing Studios film *I Believe in You* is worth seeing for its depiction of the courts, court missionaries and youthful offenders in the 1950s, for example. How useful the numerous police TV dramas are, is another matter – as they are principally made for entertainment – and are focused on the officers of the law.

Newsreels often show criminals being taken to and from court and police investigations at crime scenes. Many of these were captured by Pathe News and can be seen online (usually for a subscription fee). These capture a moment in history and can be quite eerie, especially if they show a particularly notorious villain who may seem quite ordinary, human and perhaps frightened. They may also show the notice of death being posted outside the prison gates as a crowd hastens to see it. Newsreels may also show police officers and others talking about the crime as it was being dealt with.

THE INTERNET

The current author was not brought up with the internet as a key research tool and remains sceptical of its use as a primary research mechanism. However, there is no denying that the specialist websites already mentioned can be valuable. TNA's website has a variety of useful research guides concerning criminals and prisoners, as does that of the NRS and many other record offices. However, there is much in the internet that is unreliable and repetitive. Typing in the name of a criminal, victim or crime is unlikely to bring anything up unless the crime is a significant one and those involved have some claim to merit. There are discussion boards online about the Whitechapel Murders (www.jtrforums.com) and the Rillington

Place murders, where the minutiae of each is endlessly and inconclusively discussed. There are Wikipedia articles on some crimes, but again the accuracy there is often doubtful. Other sites will repeat the relatively small amount of already published knowledge and well-known pictures of the accused, victims and others. Occasionally there may be a little new information gleaned from elsewhere, perhaps from an academic treatise which refers to the crime as part of a larger study. Some books are available for free online, such as William Bixley's informative memoir (*The Guilty and the Innocent*) as an employee of the Old Bailey in the mid-twentieth century.

THAT PERSONAL TOUCH

It is worth attempting to contact the descendants of those involved in crimes that your ancestors were also involved in. They may well have anecdotes, photographs, letters and other information that might be helpful to you in your research. John Christie's nephew was recently able to assist a researcher into his infamous uncle's life by providing photographs of Christie's father (never before seen). A researcher into double murderer Neville Heath found the daughter of his first victim happy to help with material about her life that was unavailable anywhere else and helped to draw a far more detailed picture of her than had been known of before.

Tracking down living people is always more difficult than tracking down the dead (no death certificates or wills being available to pinpoint their last known address). The website 192 is probably the best way of tracking down the address of someone living now in the UK and for a fee it can search quickly and efficiently telephone directories and electoral registers in a way that no other source can do. There is also a good book titled *People Finder* that provides excellent methods and tips for finding living people.

However, contacting people about their ancestors can be a frustrating exercise for two main reasons. Not everyone is as interested in genealogy as you may be and not everyone wants to discuss relatives whom, even if dead, were people they knew, or even if they did not know them personally, have no wish to be reminded of their personal link with them, especially if relatively recent – and several decades may count as relatively recent. A researcher alluded to above managed to contact Heath's son, who never knew his murderous father, but who had no wish to discuss him. Likewise, when I found that a triple murderer's half-sister was still living and contacted her, she told me that she had no wish to be associated with the long-dead killer in question.

However, it is certainly worth writing a tentative and polite email or letter to the individual. They may know nothing or they may not wish to discuss the matter. In which latter case, a polite reply, acknowledging their concerns and suggesting that if they change their mind it would be an honour to talk to them, is the best way. On the other hand, who knows, you may learn something of vital interest to your research and throw a whole new light on your topic of interest.

THE BANK OF ENGLAND

If an ancestor has been detected as a fraudster, there may well be relevant material at the Bank of England Archives. The Bank, naturally concerned for the soundness of the currency which it was guardian of for the government from 1694, employed agents to be vigilant and to keep tabs on potential and actual forgers. With the introduction of paper banknotes in the later 1790s as gold was less used for payments, forgery soared. Forgery of banknotes was a capital offence. Petitions from criminals can also be found in the Bank archives and are divided into whether the offence took place in London or in the provinces.

A letter from one such is as follows:

Clerkenwell March 2
Dear Sir,
I was taken into custody on suspicion of having committed a forgery on the Bank of England which I knew nothing of except for the information you gave me of the Idswell's having

158

done so and that they or some of their party had trusted with you to dispose of the plates and paper &c all I request is both for your own sake as well as mine that you will give a considerate account to the magistrates of all you know of this matter and if you contribute to the discovery I have no doubt but you will meet with a speedy Release from your confinement as the Directors of the Bank will liberally reward all persons contributing to the Detection.

I am shouted to tell you that Mrs Marshall has been taken up too. For God's sake let me interest you in the strongest manner to give all the information within your knowledge at the same time looking into that you will speak nothing but what is strictly true and by doing so you will contribute to my release and to claim upon any services in my power that I can hereafter under you and believe me to be.

Yours very sincerely

J. Marshall.

These petitions, from 1781 to 1827, are available online, in chronological order, on the Bank of England Archive's website, but are not searchable by name.

The other major resource for crime on this website are the Minutes of the Law Suits Committee from 1802 to 1908, again arranged in date order but not indexed. The committee was appointed in order to initiate and manage prosecutions in the courts on behalf of the Bank, and it mostly dealt with forgery. Entries include references to charges, assize trials, plea bargaining and responses to offers made as well as petitions by those convicted. The committee could offer rewards to informers on forgers.

There is also information about more recent cases involving currency transactions and other financial irregularities. The case of Lewis Altman & Co. is one such. This was a case in the 1970s which led to the then longest trial heard by the City Magistrates in which it was found that the said company had been committing currency fraud on a vast scale.

GALLERIES OF JUSTICE

Based at Nottingham in a former court room, the Galleries contain a whole host of material relating to criminal justice. It is in part a museum, with galleries devoted to Robin Hood (naturally enough) but also to other well-known criminals, such as Dr Crippen. There are artefacts from Wandsworth Prison's execution suite, including black caps, a trapdoor, nooses and an execution box. For the family historian, there is other material especially relating to prisons which is relevant; correspondence, transportation details and remissions. There are also archives relating to the London Police Court Mission, which was a body established to help reform evildoers; and their archives include annual reports, minute books and photographs. Archives are also held for reform schools and the Associated Societies for the Protection of Women and Children.

WELLCOME INSTITUTE FOR THE HISTORY OF MEDICINE

This institution contains a library and archives of material relevant to the history of health. It also includes much that is relevant to the family historian whose ancestor/s have been involved in crime. The library includes volumes of the *Forensic Journal*, which include articles by pathologists discussing various crimes. More uniquely there are the index cards created by top pathologist Sir Bernard Spilsbury (1877–1947) which he made out after each autopsy he performed from about 1910 to 1940. Although he is well-known for dealing with murder victims, these only made up a small number of his case files. There were far more suicides than murders, but suicides were criminal offences up to 1961, remember. Spilsbury's cards give detailed descriptions of how these corpses met their untimely deaths, in graphic and unsentimental detail. Access to the Institute's collection is via a reader's ticket.

CRUELTY TO CHILDREN

Children are particularly vulnerable to criminal acts being perpetrated against them, especially and regrettably by family members. Protecting them was, however difficult if cruelty occurred in the home (an Englishman's castle). Societies were established in the late nineteenth century to try and defend children – in Liverpool in 1883 and in London a year later. They sponsored a newspaper, *The Child's Guardian*, to highlight cases of abuse. They also brought prosecutions against cruel parents. In 1889 the NSPCC was formed and in 1899 the Prevention of Cruelty to Children Act was passed. NSPCC archives are closed to the public, but their records manager can be contacted for possible help. The Liverpool branch and other branches have often deposited archives at the appropriate CRO. These should add to the information gained from elsewhere (e.g. newspaper reports, trial records) and shed more of a light on the victims.

POLITICAL CRIME

Much of this type of offence against the state (Jacobites, Jacobins, Chartists, Luddites, Communists) can be found in quarter sessions and assize papers, but there are additional sources which may be worth checking, too. From the First World War, MI5 has been vigilant in combating internal subversion, whether Communists and Fascists in the 1920s–1980s or more modern forms of terrorism. The file series KV includes reports on such individuals. Treason trials are chiefly to be found in the KB series. Miscellaneous papers relating to sedition can be found in TS24, for the period 1732–1901. Ancestry has a listing of Suffragettes who were prosecuted from 1906 to 1914. This can be searched by name, but the details are minimal: name, date of case and magistrate's court where it was heard. These 'political' criminals are usually viewed differently by modern eyes as being heroic reformers keen to right the wrongs in the country at the time. In fact, the word 'criminal' would not be used by their many admirers. Many books, both academic and popular, have covered their activities, too.

MI5 was founded at the beginning of the twentieth century to combat internal subversion and has dealt with foes on the extreme left and right of politics, especially during the world wars. There are numerous files in series KV at TNA, which can be seen online there and are searchable by the name of the suspect. There are numerous papers concerning one Herbert Mills, for instance, who was

> apparently a person of some importance in Fascist circles as he was at a meeting in November [1939] with MOSLEY ... when co-operation between all fascist groups was discussed. It is suggested ... he may be a Gestapo agent ... he has been sneering at His Majesty's uniform. It appears desirable to ascertain the extent of his connection with important Fascist and pro-German circles.

There follows an interview with Mills, much of which concerns his views on economics, the Jews and his involvement in the Far Right Nordic League. There are also reports and letters about Mills and the meetings he attended.

DEBTORS

Until 1869 debts of over £100 were a criminal matter and could result in imprisonment. The inability of an individual, often a businessman, to meet the demands of his creditors, hence resulting in bankruptcy as assets are sold and found unable to meet debts, was a very serious matter indeed. Newspapers would often provide official notices of bankruptcy. *The London Gazette* (available freely and searchable online) included them from 1684, as did *The Edinburgh Gazette.* Perry's *Bankruptcy and Insolvent Weekly Gazette* published them from 1827. These notices would provide the name, address and occupation of the bankrupt. They might also name his or her principal creditors and would later give details of any conviction or imprisonment for debt.

TNA holds some archives relevant to imprisoned debtors. Many of these unfortunates would be sent to a number of London prisons: the Palace Court from 1630 to 1849, or the Fleet, Marshalsea, King's Bench and Queen's Prisons from 1685 to 1862. The archives for these are at TNA in series PRIS 1–11. Returns of prisoners from 1862 to 1869 can be found in B2/15–32. The Courts for the Relief of Insolvent

Debtors (1847–61) and for bankrupts from 1848 to 1862 can be located at B6/88–9, 94–6 and B6/97–8, respectively. Petitions for the release of debtors can be found at B6/45–71 for the years 1813–62. For bankruptcy outside London, there were district bankruptcy courts from 1842 to 1869, the surviving archives of which will be held at county record offices.

MISCELLANEA

Then there are the Criminal Registers, returned by each county. These (HO26) list prisoners, date and place of imprisonment prior to trial, date and result of trial, sentence and if applicable, date of execution or when transported. They also give a description of the prisoner: age, height, colour of hair and eyes, complexion. There are other details such as birthplace and occupation. There are a number of series of these records; with HO26 covering Middlesex from 1791 to 1849, HO27 which includes all England and Wales from 1805 to 1892. HO27 records fewer details about each prisoner: name, degree of literacy, age, place and date of sentence, offence and sentence. For more recent years there are the printed calendars. London cases are at CRIM9 for 1855–1949 and for elsewhere, from 1868 to 1971 at HO140. They are closed for seventy-five years. They are arranged by county and give far more information about the defendants; name, age, occupation, level of literacy, name and address of committing magistrate, offence details, verdict and sentence.

The Department of the Public Prosecutor is the organ of the state which decides whether a case should go to court and has also generated considerable archives. As with the Assizes, they are held at TNA. However they only cover a relatively small number of cases, those deemed to be of particular interest. Thus there are transcripts of some trials from 1846 to 1931 in DPP4. Some case papers relating to prosecutions from 1889 to 1992 are to be found in DPP1 and 2. Registers of cases from 1884 to 1956 are in DPP3. Most are closed for seventy-five years, especially in cases where there is doubt over the verdict or the case was never brought to court. So the DPP file covering the bank robberies which took place in Brentford in 1958 which Donald Hume was strongly suspected of but was never brought to trial, are closed for seventy-five years, whereas the DPP files for the prosecution for murder against Timothy Evans and John Christie are open for public inspection.

Those CROs which include coastal regions should have customs letter books in their holdings. These are important here because they often record smuggling, which, of course, the customs men had to deal with as part of their dangerous and arduous duties, especially in the seventeenth and eighteenth centuries before the advent of free trade in the nineteenth. Letter books of the customs officials will often refer to smugglers who had been caught and detail the goods and their value which had been confiscated. A researcher who finds a smuggler ancestor here should also check the High Court of Admiralty archives for the court case as well as the press for additional information.

This is not an exhaustive list of all the 'miscellaneous' sources which could help a researcher track down their ancestor's links with crime, but hopefully illustrates some of the sources apart from those already covered in earlier chapters.

Chapter 8

TWO CASE STUDIES

When researching ancestors who were criminals or who fell victim to crime you will usually need to look at a number of different sources outlined in this book. In order to illustrate this I will show how I researched two cases for eventual publication. Neither are related to me, but they do indicate the sources that are available to those that are or those researching ancestors who have committed crime/s or/and became victims.

A CRIMINAL

The first was John George Haigh (1909–49), acid bath murderer. In 2012–13, when I was undertaking this research, there had been already three books about him published shortly after his execution, two published decades later and a volume in the *Notable British Trials*, as well as numerous entries in compendia of crime and the subject of a recent TV film (*A is for Acid*, starring Martin Clunes). However, I decided to start by visiting TNA where I found that there was a Metropolitan Police file covering the investigation into his murder of Mrs Durand-Deacon, for which he was tried. There was also a Prison Commission file detailing Haigh's time in Wandsworth Prison in 1949, which included psychiatric reports and letters written by and to him. There were also four Home Office files about his other murders in London and Sussex.

There were six files in all – identifiable by typing 'John George Haigh' into TNA's online search engine. There was a vast array of witness statements, including those of people who did not appear at the trial, such as the brother and former husband of Mrs Henderson, his fifth victim, platonic girlfriends of his, convicts who had known him, staff at the hotel where he lived, and much, much more. There were reports by previous prison governors and staff who had known him. There was also a copy of his third statement to the police (hitherto unknown to any of the previous writers on the subject). I found myself returning to these files several times to check that I had squeezed them dry of every last drop of potential juice. There was a great deal of repetition as papers were duplicated for each of the relevant government departments.

These files had also noted his previous three convictions for theft and fraud, but gave only date, place, sentence and offence. I would need to flesh out these incidents. This I did by looking in two major sources. First, the court records: in the case of the frauds of 1934 and 1937 I found that these had been dealt with, respectively, by the Yorkshire Assizes and the Surrey Assizes. Their archives were held at TNA, too, so it was merely a case of checking the search box, not by name, but by year and by class (ASSI). These produced references to the assize court books, in chronological order, and details about the charges. In the second case, they listed the names and addresses of those people he had defrauded in a bogus shares scam, with the amounts he had taken from them and details of the shares he had offered them, with the dates in question.

All this detail was useful, but it was still quite bare bones stuff. What I needed was some newspaper reportage. Knowing when he was convicted helped, so I looked at the *Surrey Times* for the relevant date and found it referred back to the magistrates' court hearings in earlier issues. This brought about a wealth of information about how he was rumbled, how he was arrested, what happened at the court hearings and Haigh's attempt to shift the blame for the crime to another, and his final comment to the court: 'This type of fraud will, although I am sentenced, continue to be perpetrated because the engineer of that fraud is still at large'. His earlier crime was reported at length in both the *Leeds Mercury* and the *Yorkshire Post* which reported his appearance at the Leeds Petty Sessions in November and then at the assizes a month later. All these newspapers were available at the British Library newsroom.

Prison records would be the next port of call. The registers are to be found at the appropriate county record offices; in Haigh's case these are at the West Yorkshire Archives and the LMA. For the former, he was described therein as being five feet eight tall, with dark brown hair and being Church of England (contrary to his upbringing and his later professed contempt for religion). Wandsworth Prison Register noted that he had lost an inch in height, could read and write and had been born in Stamford, Rutland (actually Stamford is in Lincolnshire). The register noted that he was transferred on 14 January 1938 to Chelmsford Prison.

Given Haigh's prominence, there was much more to be found elsewhere; the *Notable Trials* volume gave a transcript of his trial at the Lewes Assizes, the *News of the World* published his memoirs, and the memoirs of various journalists, judges, psychiatrists and police officers all included references to their dealings with him. Most people's ancestors will not receive so much coverage, but some of these sources will be relevant to many researchers.

A VICTIM

The second case study is of a victim. Now victims leave fewer records behind them if they are dead; clearly no court or prison registers, no trials, no interviews in newspapers and so on. Books will often dismiss them in a very summary fashion. Yet they do not have to be wholly anonymous or at best ciphers. As with criminals, misleading and false statements can be made and are repeated subsequently.

Let us take Hectorina McKay MacLennan (1926–53), the last of John Christie's victims. Usually classed alongside his fourth and fifth victims as a prostitute, as stated at Christie's trial, this 'fact' is actually without any proof whatsoever. The major source for her short life are the statements made in the main Metropolitan Police files for John Christie, of which there are three bulky ones. The police had interviewed her sister, her brothers and two of her boyfriends (one currently serving a prison sentence for burglary) as well as the estranged wife of her most recent boyfriend, whom she had once worked for as a child minder.

Putting these statements together, one comes away with the impression that she had a miserable life before it was ruthlessly cut short, going from one low-paid job to another (cinema usherette, child minder, domestic servant) and being ultimately homeless, enduring short-term lodgings before being out on the streets. It appears she may have been married to a man in the Burmese Air Force (but the indexes to marriages do not corroborate this). Then there is Christie's statement about how he met her, inveigled her and her last boyfriend back to his house, their strange sleeping arrangements (corroborated by said boyfriend). There are also Christie's versions of how he killed her, which are unconvincing.

Newspapers were also useful. Knowing she was Scottish it made sense to check reports in *The Scotsman* just after her corpse was discovered on 25 March 1953. This produced some information about her roots in that country. A name search on the online *Daily Mirror* brought up, in 1971, an interview with her father who it appeared tried to help her return from London to Scotland, but she deceived him by telling him she had a good job and a steady romance with a young doctor. The *Sunday Pictorial*, which featured Christie's published memoir also related how he had killed her and why (a voice inside him was telling him to do so).

Fortunately Dr Camps, the pathologist on the case, wrote a lengthy study about the forensic aspects of it, including details of the post-mortems he carried out on her. He stated that there was little or no alcohol in her body, in contrast to two other victims, but like them she had been strangled and there had been intercourse at or just before death (this book can be bought at a very high price or seen for free at the British Library). To round off the picture, a search for the inquest report (held at the LMA as her death had been in London) was undertaken but it was brief in the extreme and added nothing to that already known. A search for the grave was more rewarding. Knowing that two of the people killed at 10 Rillington Place (Kensington) were, logically enough, buried in Kensington's cemetery in Gunnersbury, I rang the council's cemeteries department with the name and date and was given a plot number.

This led to finding the simple grave, which had just her name and dates on it.

I had written to a Scottish newspaper and discussed her with a journalist who subsequently made the story into a little article, with an appeal to anyone who had any anecdotes or information about her. It is more difficult to find relatives of criminals to talk, but relatives of victims often want to do so in order to put the record straight. I had one reply: a friend of the family telling me that Hectorina was 'easily led'. A relative also contacted me to state that they did not want to assist for fear of being pursued by journalists.

CONCLUSION

This book has proceeded through the many sources available for criminal ancestors and their victims. It has provided examples and locations of these sources. The reader is, therefore, better informed as to this material.

The question is, thus, what next? Criminals and victims do not often make a great advertisement of their status. The researcher may already know that one of their ancestors was involved in crime and therefore can go on to researching them using the sources mentioned. Possibly this knowledge is first hand, possibly it has been gained by finding clues on a death certificate or a military record or that on the census they are noted as being in prison or that they suddenly disappear from their usual haunts. There may be a story passed through the family that so and so was a smuggler or a bandit or involved in another nefarious activity. In all cases you will have a name and rough dates and an approximate location. Using what you know you can then seek the appropriate sources to flesh out their criminal career.

This may be a shocking experience as we find that the man always alleged to have robbed from the rich to feed his family in times of want actually stole from his equally poor neighbours. Or that their crime was a disturbing one, perhaps of a violent or sexual nature. It may be that a doctor was dropped from the *Medical Register* because he performed abortions prior to the 1960s and was found out. Or that another ancestor committed suicide. Tracing potential criminal ancestors can, therefore, be a perilous undertaking and so should only be done by those who are prepared to find the worst about someone in one's family and are able to deal with that revelation. Some can be easily detached; one man on learning that his ancestor was probably Jack the Ripper laughed it off by stating that that fact made for a more interesting family tree, but not all take that attitude.

Most of us are probably blissfully unaware of what our ancestors did apart from the usual activities of being born, marrying, having children, working and dying. Should we now suspect that each of them might have had a less than respectable life or/and was affected by crime? And if we do, should we begin to search every potential record mentioned in this book to try and find them? This is a question that only the reader can answer. A lot will depend on time, money and enthusiasm. It may well be worth checking the 'easy' sources, such as those available online and on those websites that the reader has easy access to and name checks are quick and easy to undertake.

To my mind, the key sources are newspapers, court and prison registers. Relevant parts of Ancestry such as criminal registers, transportation records and similar are also crucial. A visit to the appropriate CRO, or paying a researcher to do so, is essential. If the offence is a serious one, a visit to TNA is a probability. After that, it is a question of how much work you want to do on that family member.

The information certainly exists; not all of it, of course, as the past is fragmentary and not all of the jigsaw survives even if it was ever created in the first place. But more survives than is often thought, and crime is always of interest both to the agents of the state and to the general public and so will leave imprints on the documents of the time in a way that the law-abiding seldom do. Very few people now would have heard of Mary Kelly had she not been, in all probability, Jack the Ripper's last victim and who today would recall the mild-mannered clerk, John Christie, if he had not been a serial killer?

Crime illuminates lives which are often humdrum. Apart from their status as criminal or victim, records and other sources will provide other details about the life of an ancestor because that person will have had their life scrutinised by press, police and courts. In doing so it may well reveal information about personality, friends, family, pastimes, religion, politics, financial status and much, much more. It is not pleasant to have a criminal or a victim of crime in the family tree, but you will learn a lot more about them if they were such. If they were caught that is ...

USEFUL ADDRESSES

The National Archives
Ruskin Avenue
Kew
Surrey TW9 4DU
Tel. 020 8876 3444
Email: enquiry@tna.gov.uk
Website: www.national.archives.gov.uk/

National Records of Scotland
HM General Registry House
2 Princes Street
Edinburgh EH1 3YY
Tel. 0131 535 1314
Website: www.nrscotland.gov.uk

National Library of Wales
Abersytwyth
Ceredigion SY23 3BU
Tel. 01970 632 800
Website: gofyn@llgc.org.uk

British Library
96 Euston Road
London NW1 2BD
Tel. 01937 546060
Website: www.bl.uk

Isle of Man Public Record Office
Unit 40a

Spring Valley Industrial Estate
Douglas
Isle of Man IM2 2QS
Tel. 01624 693569
Website: http://www.gov.im/po

Isle of Wight Record Office
26 Hillside
Newport PO30 2EB
Tel. 01983 823820
Website: https://www.iwight.com
Email: record.office@iow.gov.uk

Jersey Archives
Clarence Road
St Helier
Tel. 01534 833300
Website: http://www.jerseyheritage.org

Borthwick Institute for Archives
University of York
Heslington
York YO10 5DD
Tel. 01904 321166
Email: borthwick-institute@york.ac.uk

Wellcome Institute for the History of Medicine
183 Euston Road
London NW1 2BE
Tel. 020 7611 2222
Email: info@wellcomecollections.org.uk

Galleries of Justice Museum
High Pavement
Nottingham NG1 1HN
Tel. 0115 952 0555
Email: info@galleriesofjustice.org.uk

Bank of England Archives
Threadneedle Street
London EC2R 8AH
Tel. 020 7601 33388
Email: archive@bankofengland.co.uk

Berkshire Record Office
9 Coley Road
Reading RG1 6AF
Tel. 0118 937 5132

BIBLIOGRAPHY

E Beckman, *Victims of Piracy: The Admiralty Courts, 1575–1678* (1979).

I Bridgeman and C Emsley, *A Guide to the Archives of the Police Forces of England and Wales* (1990).

C Chapman, *Sex, Sin and Probate* (1997).

M Cole, *Law and Society: An Introduction to Sources for Crime and Legal History from 1800* (1996).

I Edwards, *A Catalogue of Star Chamber Proceedings Relating to Wales* (1929).

M Ellis, *Using Manorial Records* (1997).

Y Fitzmaurice, *Army Deserters from His Majesty's Service* (1988).

J S W Gibson, *Quarter Sessions Records for Family Historians: A Select List* (1995).

J S W Gibson and C Rogers, *Coroners' Records in England and Wales* (2000).

P D A Harvey, *Manorial Records* (1999).

D Hawkings, *Criminal Ancestors: A Guide to Historical Records in England and Wales* (1996)

D Hawkings, *Bound for Australia* (2012).

G Oram and J Putkowski, *Death Sentences Passed by the Military Courts of the British Army, 1914–1925* (1998).

R Paley, *Using Criminal Records* (2001).

R Paley and S Fowler, *Family Skeletons: Exploring the Lives of Our Disreputable Ancestors* (2005).

G Parry, *A Guide to the Records of Great Sessions in Wales* (1995).

G Parry, *Launched to Eternity: Crime and Punishment, 1700–1900* (2001).

J Putkowski, *British Army Mutineers, 1914–1922* (1998).

D Thomas, *Beggars, Cheats and Forgers* (2014).

J Wade, *Tracing Your Criminal Ancestors* (2009).

INDEX